Memories of
Gateshead

by Kathleen Harrison

Introduction

I was brought up in the 1950s in the Bensham and Saltwell area of Gateshead. In a time when there was a great sense of community. Everyone looked out for each other ... and a cup of sugar could be borrowed. When the kitchen was the scullery and the toilet or netty was at the bottom of the backyard.

The streets were full of children playing and they had such freedom to wander around the area to school or even the park.

Our family wasn't well off financially – which family was during these years? The years after the Second World War was a time of austerity with rationing of food and clothes and other items. Having said this there was always food on the table at every meal in our home and clothes to wear, even if they might have been hand-me-downs. There were plenty of corner shops and bigger stores in the High Street. We as children and the grown-ups entertained ourselves with singing around the piano, dancing, card games, the wireless and much more. This was a time when the holidays were days spent in the park ... a day

Kathleen Harrison at the door of St Chad's Church, Bensham in 2016.

in the country ... a day trip to the seaside ... or camping on Ryton Willows.

I have lived in other places but it is Gateshead that played a big part in shaping my life and who I am.

You can take the girl out of Gateshead
but you cannot take Gateshead out of the girl.

Kathleen Harrison

Previous page: Gateshead High Street around 1960.

Front cover: The author's gran and grandfather in 1905. The author's parents and aunts and uncles at a family wedding. Children at Prior Street School who took part in a dance around the maypole in Saltwell Park to celebrate the Coronation in 1953.

Back cover: St Chad's Church, Bensham in 2016. Saltwell Park House.

Copyright Kathleen Harrison 2016

First published in 2016 by

Summerhill Books
PO Box 1210, Newcastle-upon-Tyne NE99 4AH

ISBN: 978-1-911385-05-9

email: summerhillbooks@yahoo.co.uk

www.summerhillbooks.co.uk

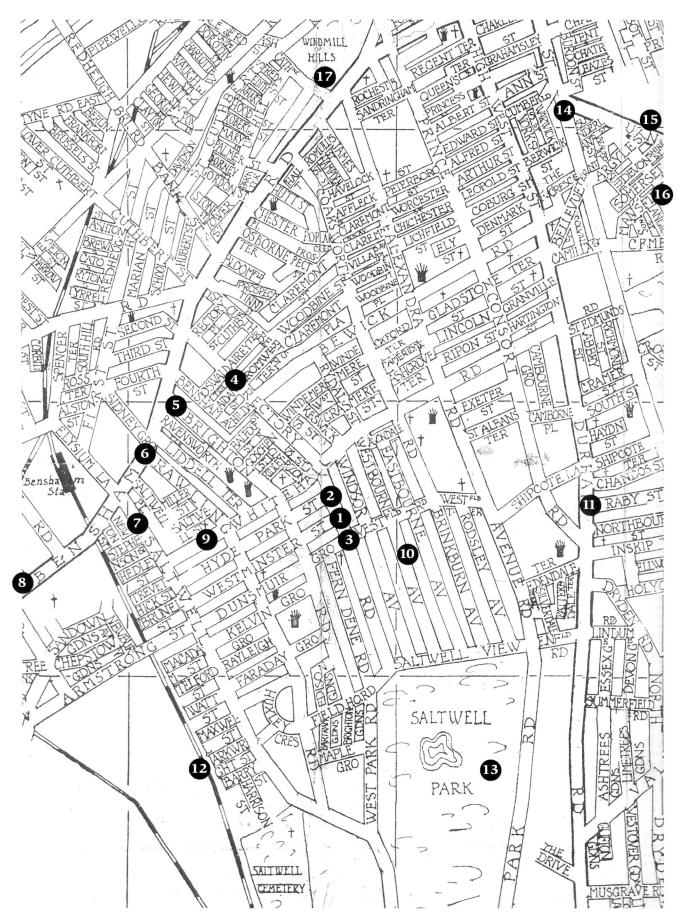

A map of the area of Gateshead that was my world. 1 Westminster Street. 2 Hyde Park Street.
3 Dunsmuir Grove. 4 Rectory Road. 5 Brighton Road. 6 Rawling Road. 7 Saltwell Road.
8 Bensham Road. 9 Whitehall Road. 10 The Avenues. 11 Raby Street. 12 Arkwright Street.
13 Saltwell Park. 14 High Street. 15 Argyle Street. 16 Langdon Street. 17 Windmill Hills.

Life at Home

'I'll take you home again, Kathleen …'

I was named Kathleen after the song *I'll take you home again, Kathleen* made famous by Joseph Locke and Bing Crosby. My dad would sing it to me – and his name just happened to be 'Tom Jones'.

I was born on 28th March 1947 during a harsh, snowy winter. Back then, most babies were home births and my aunty, my mam's sister, delivered me. My aunty did all of my mum's deliveries. 'Why is Aunty Doreen here?' I would ask, as I grew older, at each of the births of my siblings. I was child number three out of seven children in a family of five girls and two boys. 'She brings the babies,' I was told. So I assumed she had found each baby under the gooseberry bush, because that's where they came from, didn't they?

Back then, at least in our house, babies seemed to always be delivered in the front bedroom,

My dad – Tom Jones.

'I'll take you home again, Kathleen' by Bing Crosby.

probably because this was a big square room with a very large fireplace with roaring, red, crackling coals. The fire kept the room warm and, using a big pan or kettle on the red hot coals, boiled the water that was needed. (That's what they did is those days with no running hot water in a bathroom next door.) There weren't posh carpets on the floor either. The floor was covered in brown patterned 'oilcloth' as it was called (the forerunner to linoleum), with a proggy mat over it. This was a mat made by my mam. In other homes maybe by dad.

Me as a baby when I was five months old.

Mats were made out of old clothes, usually suits, because they were hard wearing. They would have been passed down from father to son etc and, when finished with, cut into strips to be used for the proggy mat. Clothes were always passed down from child to child. Some of mine would have belonged to my older sister or even an older cousin. They knew how to recycle back then.

Back to the mat. It would be thrown somewhere on the floor and was moveable so could be kicked aside, so any mess from births was easily cleaned up. There was plenty of room around the big bed for those involved in the birth to move around.

The other bedroom, what we called the back bedroom, was much smaller. I cannot remember a fireplace in this room, but I can remember sleeping in either of these bedrooms. There would always be two beds in the room occupied by me and my siblings. We slept four in a bed, two at the top and two at the bottom. The oldest sibling would be in a single bed and this was either my elder sister or my elder brother. My eldest brother, Allan, was the only boy in our family for a long time. My younger baby brother, Bryan, arrived in 1955. As my older brother grew up he got his own bedroom – sleeping in the cupboard under the stairs! The baby was always with Mam and Dad in their bedroom. For us, and many other families, a baby's first bed was one of the drawers out of the 'tall boy' as it was called. This was a brown, heavy, wooden chest of drawers that stood in the alcove next to the chimney breast in the front bedroom.

The bedding was always sheets and blankets and an eiderdown thrown over them. In the winter we got a hot water bottle at the beginning of the night, but we kept each other warm sleeping in spoon position. If anyone moved they got shouted at by another child.

Our toilet was 'down the yard'. So if we wanted to go, it was the china pot under the bed. Again oilcloth was a useful floor covering for obvious reasons.

I grew up during the 1950s at 115 Westminster Street in Gateshead, in what is now called a Tyneside flat. The entrance was a green front door with the street number at the top and a letter box in the middle. The door opened on to a small square alcove, with a heavy outdoor mat on the floor to wipe our feet. There was then another door leading along a short passage which was a dark place. The only light, peeping out into the passage, came through the little glass windows above each door. The passage floor was covered with oilcloth and a long runner of a mat on top of it.

'Our street'.

Along this passage on the left was the front bedroom and at the end of the passage, facing the front door, was the door to the back bedroom. On the left, after bedroom one, was the kitchen. It was called a kitchen, not a lounge or a living room. Opposite the kitchen door in the passage, there was a cupboard under the stairs which led to the upstairs flat.

The kitchen was the heart of family life. It housed a large wooden table with chairs and I think a long form for us bairns to sit on. There was a settee against the inside wall, close enough to the very large, black-leaded fireplace. This fireplace went half way up the chimney wall. At each side of the fire there was an oven either with a door or just shelves. Over the fire there was a hook hanging down. A pan or kettle could be hooked on to it to boil water or cook food. Next to the chimney breast at one side there was a cot and there always seemed to be a cot there with all those babies and toddlers – five girls and two boys. However, I remember eventually, years later, a piano took over this spot. On the other side of the chimney breast was a small cupboard hiding behind the armchair and the scullery door when it was open. There was always a big fireguard around the fire. Often there were clothes hanging around it, drying in the winter.

There was a large radio, or wireless as it was called, sitting on top of a sideboard. This big brown sideboard was tall enough to reach the windowsill of the one and only big sash window in the room. The window not only gave us views into the backyard, but also brought daylight from outside into the room. This was ideal as there was no electricity in our home. I'm not sure if there was any electricity in any of the houses in Westminster Street.

The source of light in the kitchen was from a gas mantle which hung from the centre of the ceiling. I remember Dad climbing on to a chair and pulling a little chain which hung down, turning on the gas. He would strike a match and hold it against the white mantle. There was a gas mantle in each of the bedrooms.

Through the kitchen was the scullery. This was where dishes were washed, water boiled, washing done and food cooked. The scullery was small in size. There was a window next to the back door which went out into the yard. Next to the door was a white sink with a cold water tap. I remember when washing the dishes we used water from the cold tap and hot water from the kettle. There was a cooker in the scullery and this was black and white with a four burner hob and an oven beneath.

Westminster Street in 1958.

In the corner of the scullery stood a grey corrugated tub with a lid on it and a tap on the side near the top. This was our boiler standing on a concrete plinth. It had a small gas pipe underneath which, when lit, produced a powerful flame that could heat up the tin boiler and in turn the cold water in it. It must have taken a long time to do this and the water was used for bathing and for washing clothes. When hot enough it was drained into the grey corrugated tin bath which was placed in front of the fire every Friday night.

As Dad would say: 'You have a bath whether you need one or not!' We all took turns in this bath water – oldest first, youngest last or was it the other way around? I would laugh and be glad I was child number three as the family grew because the last would be just as dirty when they came out as they were when they went in. We used brown carbolic soap and the smell has stayed with me forever.

Friday night was also a night for putting the cream on our heads if we had head lice and it was left on all weekend. Mam

Me as a five year old.

would check us on the Sunday night with our heads over a newspaper and, using a nit comb, the special comb for the job, she would comb through. This would remove the now dead nit eggs from our hair. Our hair was then washed and this got rid of the cream so we would be clean for school the next day.

Water was heated in the boiler on a Monday because this was washing day. Memories abound on this because we, the girls, would always help when we did not have to go to school. Clothes would be put into the 'poss' tub, which I think was also the boiler, along with OMO cloths, washing stuff or the carbolic soap. Mam would let us girls take turns in using the poss stick. I would push it up and down, possing the wet things and Mam would tell me when to stop. She would pull the now heavy, wet clothes out of the water. Then she would slowly pull and push them between the two rollers of the mangle standing behind the tub. We bairns would each take turns with the winding handle at the side of the mangle that turned the rollers. The clothes came through and out the other end. That's as much as we young 'uns wanted to do.

Mam gathered all the washed clothes together and she called to us 'bring the pegs and help me hang out.' I called the pegs 'dolly pegs' because their shape to me was like a doll with its arm down by its side. We handed the pegs to Mam and she pegged the clothes on the line to dry in the backyard. Sheets and towels were hungout on the lines across the back lane. Each family had their own clothes line strung across the lane from one side to the other. The backyard was for clothes, with two lines from one end of the yard to the other. Woe betide us lot if Mam caught us having fun running through the clothes as they were drying either in the yard or the lane.

The backyard wasn't that big to hang clean washing but it was ok. In the yard there was also the outside toilet, the coalhouse and a shed. This meant there was not a lot of space left to play in the yard on wash day. At the far side of the yard, next to the back door into the lane, was the netty as it was called. It was a small place but big to me. It was brick-built from ground to top and the floor was concreted. The toilet was a big white thing with a brown toilet lid and it was 'a rite of passage' to be able to climb on by myself

An advert from Northern Laundries showing the hard work at home on a wash day – with a poss tub, wash board, mangle and clothes line (and the days before health and safety).

without help. The flushing cistern was up high near the roof and the rope to flush it was very long with a knot in the end to hold on to while pulling. Again for a 6, 7, 8 or even 9 year old it was a challenge. Toilet paper (oh toilet paper!) meant you always had plenty to read as it was newspaper cut up into squares and hung on a nail within reach. It was a child's job to cut the paper into squares and hang them.

On the other side of the back door into the lane was the coalhouse. It had a door on it and, when open, coal stayed behind the makeshift bunker until shovelled into a bucket and taken to use on the fire in the kitchen. The coal man came every week and, lifting from the lorry sacks of coal on his back, opened a hatch from the back lane side and tipped the sack into the coalhouse where it stayed till needed. This activity fascinated me – the lifting, carrying and dropping the coal into our coalhouse.

At the other side of the backyard was Dad's shed, probably not large but big to me. The shed was where Dad repaired all of our shoes and he had all the tools – a cobbler's last and special sharp knives. We were always being warned about the dangers of touching. There was plenty of shoe leather (which I can still smell) and tacks to mend shoes. It was cheaper than buying new ones. I remember we had sandals in the summer made by Dad and these sandals were special to me – I wore them with pride.

This was home to us seven children and Mam and Dad and sometimes a cat with kittens. Now and again there might be a dog, a stray, but maybe because of the overcrowding and food rationing, dogs didn't stay long. But I stayed a long time. This was to be my home during my formative years which lasted until I was eleven years old going on twelve.

An advert for J. Batey coal merchant – 'We deliver to any part of Gateshead'.

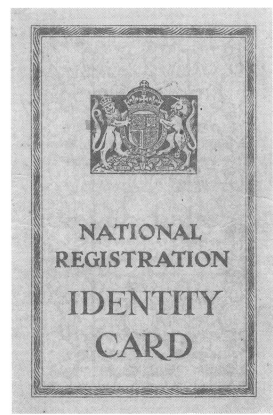

Above: An Identity Card – carried by everyone from 1939 to 1952.

Right: Mam and Dad's details on their Identity Cards.

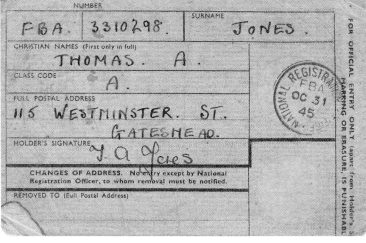

Family Memories

Mam and Dad were from large families. Mam's mother married twice. Her first husband was killed in the First World War – they had four sons. From the second marriage, there was four daughters so eight children in all.

Mam was born in Claremont Place, just off Coatsworth Road, near to 'The Windmill Hills'. I remember going to the hills with her and my sisters to play when we were in that area. There were different buildings on the hills and I think a school. It was also a place me and Mam would walk across to go down to the West Street or High Street shopping.

Dad was one of seven children and his mother also married twice. She and her first husband met while living at 19 and 20 Park Lane. They married at St Edmund's Chapel on the High Street in Gateshead. This Granda was killed, at aged 27, in a freak accident in a brick yard in Stockton. A runaway truck holding bricks ran him down.

There were five children – three girls and two boys to support. Gran moved back to Gateshead after this and the family lived in Berwick Street. She met and married her second husband and together they had two daughters so seven children in all. It is her second husband that I think of as Granda. They lived in 113 Westminster Street for a number of years during the Second World

Mam and Dad with my aunts and uncles at a family wedding at St John's Church on Rawling Road. Front row: Aunty Betty, Aunty Elsie, Aunty Doreen, Mam. Back row: Uncle Frank, Uncle Fred, Uncle Sid, Dad.

War. This is where my parents lived for a while during the war and Mam stayed there while Dad was away. Eventually Mam and Dad moved to 115 Westminster Street, where my Aunty Mary and Uncle Chris lived before they moved to Rectory Road, beside Saltwell Park. One of Dad's sisters and her family eventually lived upstairs at 117 Westminster Street. Thus there was always family living in Westminster Street for a long time.

Eventually my paternal grandparents also moved to Rectory Road at the Whitehall Road end. Living with them was my Aunty Evelyn and Uncle Joe and my cousin Heather. Gran and Granda living on Rectory Road is where my memories of this time come from.

Left: Grandma and Granda (my dad's parents) in the backyard in Park Lane, on the day of their wedding in 1905.

Below: Park Lane where Grandma and Granda lived before I was born. This photo shows the street in 1942.

A Close Knit Community

On Sunday mornings we would visit my grandparents. I would watch Granda getting ready – polishing his shoes and cleaning his bowls for his bowls game at Saltwell Park. On these Sunday visits Gran gave us bairns a glass of pop which was a very rare thing. My cousin Heather loved Sunday visits from her cousins because that was also the only day she got a glass of pop, as we all did as it was such a treat back then. I think it was Fentiman's pop, delivered to the front door by the pop man. I believe the Fentiman's factory was at the bottom of Bensham Road.

Saltwell Park where Granda played bowls on a Sunday.

At the back of Rectory Road, which for me was the back lane, there was an ice cream shop. I don't remember the name, if there was one, and it could have been just a person selling homemade stuff from their backyard. It looked just like a stable door, with the top half opening, where we handed over a penny of our pocket money to buy delicious ice lollies.

Aunty Elsie (cousin Peter Annable's Mam) going to do her weekly shop with her curlers in 1955.

There was always a relative for us to visit or sometimes they visited us in Westminster Street. We were surrounded by family – at the Saltwell Park end of Rectory Road lived Aunty Mary and Uncle Chris with three of my cousins. Some relatives lived up the Avenues in the Shipcote area. Others lived off Saltwell Road, near to the Palladium Picture House. My Aunty Doreen and Uncle Sid lived in Saltwell Street behind Rawling Road Methodist Church. In Argyle Street lived Aunty Elsie, Uncle Fred and my cousin Peter. In Langdon Street, behind the High Street, lived Aunty Lily, Uncle Billy, Janice and Gwenny, who eventually lived in Langdon Street after she married. My Aunt and Uncle and cousin Janice moved to Brinkburn Avenue where another of Dad's sisters lived with her family.

My Mam's oldest brother Alex and his wife and my cousins lived in Raby Street just off Durham Road near Gateshead's Cenotaph and the Shipcote Picture House.

I have fond memories of visiting my aunts, uncles and cousins either with Mam or Dad or eventually, as I grew older, my sisters and I would visit on our own. We had fun playing with our cousins in their backyards or the street or just wandering to the park or cemetery to play.

Everyone looked out for everyone else and it was a safe place for children. Adults knew each other and they knew each other's children. We had a lot of friends from the cousins in the family and school friends to neighbours friends so therefore it was a close knit community. We as children had a lot of freedom because of this and where ever we went, along streets to Saltwell Park or school and anywhere else in between, we were safe. If anyone, either stranger or child bothered us, there was probably a cousin, an aunty, a family friend or a neighbour looking out for us, or there was a family door to knock on for help.

The Neighbourhood

We lived in the Bensham/Saltwell area of Gateshead – between Saltwell Park and Bensham Road. Our flat was what now are called 'Tyneside Flats'. They had two bedrooms upstairs and two bedrooms downstairs. The flats were in long rows of cobbled streets that started from Rectory Road and went down to Brighton Road. Another row of flats went down to Rawling Road. Finally a third row of flats ended at Saltwell Road. The streets in this area were based on a matrix grid system with roads going across them – Rectory Road, Brighton Road, Rawling Road and Saltwell Road.

There was what was called the top, the middle and the bottom of Westminster Street. Our flat was in the middle block. We just called it 'our street'. The rows of streets adjacent to Westminster Street were Hyde Park Street, Dunsmuir Grove and Kelvin Grove. This area became my playground with our school on the corner of Brighton Road and Whitehall Road.

A postcard view of Bensham Road. It is a bit before my time but it does show one of the area's many corner shops.

Corner Shops

There was a 'corner shop' on each of the four corners of our street looking on to Brighton Road. On the corner just up from where we lived there was a green grocer shop, owned by Mr and Mrs Stephenson. On the opposite corner of the street was Glendenning's the pawn shop. This shop had a strange smell and I wasn't keen on going with Mam to this shop. There were all sorts of items to look at – watches, fob watches, jewellery and clothes. There were also other kinds of household items but I didn't stay long enough to have a good look around. I would go outside to play.

Over time, I think towards the end of the 1950s, maybe 1957, Glendenning's became Alice Long's gown shop. It was a ladies fashion shop and was where I went to buy the ribbon for my hair so a much better shop for a little girl to visit.

On the opposite side of the green grocers across Brighton Road there was the Co-op or 'Store' as it was known. On the opposite corner to the Co-op was Forster's fried fish shop. These were the main shops I visited in my small world.

An advert for Alice Long's gown shop from 1957.

Messages

My Mam would often send me 'with a message' – a shopping list wrapped around money, either coins or paper.

'Kath, go get me a message. Mind hand it to Mr Stephenson and do not open it. There's a good girl,' she would say.

And off I would trot. I loved going into the green grocers because it smelt so good with all the fruit and vegetables. Mr Stephenson would put together the items on the list and place them in the bag I brought with me. He would then wrap the change in the piece of paper with the list on it and give it all back to me. He was a good man. Sometimes he would tell me to take an apple for myself from the wooden boxes on the floor filled with them.

If mam sent me a message to the fish shop she would also give me an empty lemonade bottle. 'Ask Mr Forster for the money off the bottle,' she would say.

I really didn't like going for this message. I would get to the little counter after standing in a queue for a long time between all of the grown-ups. 'Me Mam sent this message and can I have the money off the bottle, please?' I would say looking at him with doleful eyes.

He would look at the bottle, then at me and say: 'Money off the bottle? I can't see any money on the bottle?' as he turned it around and around.

I would stand there just staring at his white apron tied around his waist at the front, never sure if I would get the money. Then he would hand over a 'paper'.

'There you are, the money off the bottle and your Mam's change,' he would say.

I breathed a sigh of relief. He did this every time and probably with all the bairns who went into his shop – he might have been smiling as he joked but I never saw it.

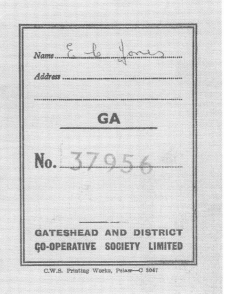

My mam's Co-op dividend book.

The Store

Going a message to the 'Store' was the best challenge. Each customer had a number and everything bought over time was purchased against this number. This number ensured the customer got their 'dividend' which was an amount of money given back to the customer – a percentage of what was spent over time. When the goods were put together and the amount written on a small stub in a book the assistant would say: 'What's your Mam's number?' – Proudly I would reply: '37956.'

I would say it over and over in my head on the way to the shop in case I forgot it so when asked it would tumble out of my mouth.

The Co-op Store had a biscuit smell from the broken biscuits which could be bought at a reduced price. I loved the taste of these and the smell of them alongside the other smells of the bacon, cheese and butter sold in this shop. There was always the smell of sawdust.

Behind the counter, where the shop assistant put together the items from the message, were sacks of sugar or flour sitting on the sawdust covered floor. Food products were not prepacked and were all weighed out as needed. I would watch as the assistant scooped the sugar or flour out of the sacks and tipped it from the scoop on to the scales. These scales had a shallow dish on one side where the flour or sugar would be placed while the other smaller dish was where the weight (1oz, ½ lb or 1 lb) would be placed. With the flour or sugar on the dish on one side of the scales the assistant placed the weight on the dish on the other side. If the dish on either side balanced then the right quantity had been reached. The assistant took the dish from the scales and tipped its contents into a paper bag. For a child it was so fascinating to watch.

An advert for the dividend from Gateshead Co-operative Society.

CO-OPERATIVE STORES AND HALL. WHITEHALL ROAD, GATESHEAD 574

The Co-operative Stores and Hall on Whitehall Road.

Cheese or butter came in big slabs, resting on the benches behind the counter. The assistant used a wire to cut a piece of butter or cheese from the large slab. She would then place the piece on the scales and using the weights measure what was required.

Bacon was sliced as needed. The butcher behind the counter would place a large piece of ham on to the bacon slicer close to the blade. I'm not sure how it worked but the butcher held the ham in place while the slicer did the work.

Eggs were placed into brown paper bags and handed to the customer. Usually all the messages on the list were placed into the shopping bag I always took with me.

KITCHEN PEDAL BINS Were 42/6' — NOW **18/11**	GIRLS SHOES, sizes 11 to 1 .... **12/6** BOYS' SHOES, size 4 .... **16/11** CHILD'S SHOES, sizes 1 to 6 .... **3/11** Travellers' Samples — Genuine Bargains	*READYMADES DEPT.* GENTS D.B. SUITS .... £5/10/0 BOYS' SUITS .... £1/15/0 BOYS' JERKINS 16/6
CARPET DEPT. COCO MATTING, 27" Wide, per yard **2/6** 5% REDUCTION ON ALL CARPETS, RUGS AND LINOS	*DRUGS DEPT.* ODDMENTS OF FANCY GOODS at Greatly Reduced Prices	*TAILORING DEPT.* 10% REDUCTION ON ALL SUITS, COSTUMES AND OVERCOATS ORDERED BEFORE JANUARY 31

EVERY CUSTOMER CAN FIND A REAL BARGAIN !!!
○○○○○○○○○○○○○○○○○○○○○○○○○○○○ DIVIDEND TIME SALE ○○○○○○○○○○○○○○○○○○○○○○○○○○

UNDERWEAR DEPT. THE LATEST SHORTIE PYJAMAS .... 10/- NYLON NIGHTDRESSES, Reduced to ... £1 BRASSIERES from .... 4/6 WOMEN'S VESTS AND PANTEES from 2/4	*CHILDREN'S DEPT.* A FEW ONLY NAP COATS, reduced from £5 .... 29/11 BABY SHAWLS from .... 6/11 CHILDREN'S DRESSES from .... 10/11 GYM DRESSES, asstd. sizes and cols. 19/11	*HOUSEHOLD DRAPERY* UNION BLANKETS, 70 x 90 .... 37/6 80 x 100 .... 39/11 RUG CANVAS, reduced from 7/11 yd to 1/6 CURTAIN MATERIAL 36" from .... 2/9 48" from 3/6
MANTLES DEPT. LADIES' COATS from .... 29/11 LADIES' DRESSES, assorted sizes from 14/11 JUNIOR MISS AND CHILDREN'S COATS from .... 14/11 LADIES' COSTUMES from 45/11	*MILLINERY DEPT.* HATS at 5/- 7/6 10/- 15/- 20/- ALL MODEL HATS REDUCED **GATESHEAD** **CO—OP** JACKSON STREET	*SKIRT DEPT.* SKIRTS, all sizes .... 24/11 LADIES' WOOL CARDIGANS from .. 22/11 LADIES' LUMBER JACKETS from .. 22/11 LADIES' WOOL JUMPERS from ...... 17/6 *HOSIERY DEPT.* F.F. NYLONS, 30 Denier .... 4/11 SEMI-FASHIONED LISLE HOSE .... 1/11 *WOOL DEPT.* D.K. WOOL .... 1/1 COCKTAIL WOOL, reduced from 2/4 to 1/6

An advert for the Gateshead Co-op on Jackson Street from 1958.

Unsliced bread came from the bakers. This shop was up the Avenues and I remember going with Mam on a Saturday to get bread. It was quite a walk up the Avenues to the bakery but well worth it because the smell of freshly baked bread, meat squares and all sorts of baked food was wonderful.

During this time there was processed and sliced bread which could be bought. The bread was from Hendees, a small bakery on Lobley Hill Road, at the bottom of Bensham Road. There was also Sunblest Bread produced by Hunters the Bakers on the Team Valley Trading Estate.

Another shop I visited when I was young was the 'paper shop' at the top of Dunsmuir Grove on Brighton Road. I think it might have been called Robson's. On a Saturday, after tea, about 5 o'clock or maybe 6 o'clock, I would go and get 'The Pink' for Dad. It held all the football scores from the games played on a Saturday afternoon and I had to rush home with it because it was needed to check the scores against the football pools piece of paper. I knew it was important because if we won it meant we would be rich.

Left: An advert for the Evening Chronicle's 'Pink' that had all the latest sports results.

St Chad's Church

On the opposite side of Westminster Street, towering over us all, was St Chad's Church. The church went down to the end of our street and continued along Rawling Road to Dunsmuir Grove. I have fond memories of St Chad's Church. Mam was the caretaker and I would help her with some of the jobs she did. We always went into the church from the little door (known as the Vestry door) at the side. Just inside the door, hanging on the wall, was a long picture of Jesus. I think I remember he was dressed in a white robe and it was tied with a blue, rope-type belt. On his head was a crown of thorns. In the picture he was standing outside a door, knocking on it with his right hand. In his left hand he was holding a brightly lit lamp. The picture was called 'The Light of the World' and it kept me on the straight and narrow (mostly) as a child.

One night there was a knocking on our front door. It was dark and I was in bed. The house was silent and I became so scared at hearing the knock that I thought to myself that it was Jesus knocking. He had come for me as I must have been naughty that day. I knew that Jesus had a hard time 'suffering the children to come to him' – so he had to suffer me. I lay perfectly still until I went back to sleep.

Years later I found out from Dad that he had one of the workman knock on the door as a morning alarm for him to get up to go to work at Osram Lamps on the Team Valley Trading Estate. This man would knock on doors as he came back up Westminster Street after night shift and was known as the 'knocker-upperer'.

Inside St Chad's Church.

'The Light of the World' – a picture that hung in St Chad's Church.

Our Allan was one of the choristers at St Chad's. As I got a bit older I would go along by myself to the morning services to listen to him singing. I would slip in unnoticed and sit in the pews near the back. I remember one time, but thought it might have been several times, there was a procession of the clergy walking down the central isle. I think it might have been the vicar at the front of this procession who would be carrying and swinging a globe. Smoke would be coming out of the globe and the smell to me was too much and I had to leave the church because I felt sick.

St Chad's Church. Bensham. In 1952 the Gateshead Post described the church as 'one of the most beautiful in Gateshead'.

Then there were the Christenings. People walked to the church with one of the godparents carrying the baby. Christening bread was given away and this was generally a buttered teacake wrapped in greaseproof paper. Inside the teacake would be money – a coin either a sixpence, shilling etc. As the family walked down the street to the church, the christening bread was given to a child. If the baby was a boy it went to girl. If baby was a girl the bread was given to a boy. I, my siblings and some of my cousins, were all christened in St Chad's.

There were also the weddings. These were glamorous occasions to little girls, watching it all beside the main door of the church where the photographs were taken. Of course there was a 'Hoy oot' when we all shouted out as the wedding car carrying the bride and her father went down the street. The bride's father would throw money out of the car windows and we scrambled on the cobbled road collecting as much as we could.

In previous decades my Aunty Evelyn and Uncle Joe were marred at the church as was my Aunty Jessie and Uncle Alf. St Chad's holds a lot of memories for my family.

The cross outside of St Chad's Church.

Corpus Christi

When I got told off by Mam, especially if this happened after school, I would 'run away'. I didn't go very far, only to Corpus Christi Church School on Dunsmuir Grove. I remember there was a little air raid shelter or some sort of small building attached to the side wall of the school. I could climb up on to the flat top and, lying on my tummy, looked over the wall into the playground where the girls were playing netball. Eventually I would go home because I was hungry – I never missed a meal!

School Days

In the 1950s there were three intakes a year to school – Easter, Summer and Winter terms. I was born at the end of March so my school days began after Easter in April 1952. The next intake was at the beginning of September after the summer holidays. The winter term began after Christmas in January.

Brighton Avenue School

The school I attended from the age of five was Brighton Avenue School which was at the cross roads of Whitehall Road and Brighton Grove, almost all the way along to Bensham Road. It was a Nursery, Infant, Junior and Senior school all on the one site. Mam would have taken me the first day for a 9 o'clock start. After that I went to school sometimes with my older sister, or our Allan, who were older by about 3 or 4 years. They would have been in the junior part of the school. Older bairns in families looked after younger ones. Mam could stand at our corner and see us along the back lanes to school. She had a clear view all the way to the school gates on Whitehall Road. There were no cars then, at least only one or two on the main roads. In June 1952 another sister was born and Mam would still have three children under five to look after. It wasn't easy for her. I would go home at 4 o'clock on my own, or if our Allan came past the infants he would walk me back.

The first week or two I didn't settle well. I went home at dinner time for a cooked meal, as did my two older siblings. I think only children who got a free meal stayed in school. During the morning and afternoon sessions there was a play time and I would go home. I don't know why. I can only think it was because that's what I did at dinner time. It wasn't far to go home through the back lanes and if I ran, which I did because the lanes were quiet, it was quicker. School gates back then, at least in our school, were never locked. Mam would have a fit and tell me off all the way back to school. I did this for about two weeks.

My class photograph from Brighton Avenue School in 1958.

On a Friday, I remember we were allowed to take a toy into school in the afternoon. After dinner time on a particular Friday I had my toy in hand ready to go back. I must have decided I wasn't going to go back that Friday and I ran down the street. Mam ran after me ranting and raving. She finally caught me and smacked me on the backs of my legs. She took me to school and after that I went without a fuss.

The classrooms went around the hall and within each room there were rows and rows of desks. There was a blackboard on an easel where the teacher wrote with her white chalk which she rubbed out with a blackboard rubber. The desks were generally twin desks. The lid lifted open to show a space where I could keep my books either for writing or arithmetic, as well as my pencils or pens. In the junior school there were ink-pots in a little well at the top of the desks. I used ink when we were taught to do real writing with a fountain pen. We had to sit on a little form beside someone.

My friends from school were Mary McCloud, and others whose names I have forgotten. I also played with some of the boys, again names escape me. My cousin Sidney went to my school so there was always someone to play with.

We learnt what was called the three Rs – 'riting, reading and rithmatic'. Children faced the front of the class looking at the teacher. We listened intently, at least appeared to. If we talked or made any fuss we got shouted at. If our behaviour was really bad we might get smacked with a leather strap or caned. Corporal punishment was the thing to do to keep children in line.

PE

There was Physical Education – PE as it was called. This took place in the big hall. We didn't have kits of shorts and t-shirts so we did PE in our vests and navy blue knickers for the girls and vest and underpants for the boys. This was also in our bare feet. We would run around the hall and stop when teacher blew the whistle. We carried bean bags on our heads as we walked carefully, trying not to drop them off. Teacher would say: 'Walk tall, hold your shoulders back and stick out your chest.'

She would sometimes say to us girls: 'When you grow up you will have lovely unrounded shoulders and you will walk tall and elegantly.'

I didn't have a clue what she meant but I always did as I was told. I didn't want to get into trouble.

There were the wooden horses which we had to line up and take a turn at jumping over. Scary stuff as the horses seemed so tall and big when I was around six and seven.

Health

The school doctor came regularly. We had to take turns when our name was called out in class then go into the hall and sit on the forms till it was our turn. The school nurse would help us strip off down to our knickers ready to be examined by the doctor. He used his cold stethoscope to check our chests and backs. We had to stick out our tongues for him to look at as well as turn our hands over so he could look at the front and backs of them. He also looked at our feet. Our height and weight was taken and our eyesight checked.

There was also the school dentist who came regularly and looked at our teeth. I remember one time I had to go to the dentist in the Greenesfield Clinic to get some of my teeth taken out. Our Elizabeth went there at times to have her eyes seen to.

Then there was the nurse who examined our heads for lice or nits as we called them. She was known as 'Nitty Nora the dicky explorer'. It was all so embarrassing even for a child. Heaven forbid she found anything in my head.

I do remember at home, on a regular basis, all of us bairns had to have a DDT treatment. This must have meant one of us had head lice.

Shephard's department store stocked all the uniform you would need for school.

16

Extracts from Brighton Avenue School Log Book

July 1957, Junior School: Scottish Children's Theatre.

3rd November 1957: Book Exhibition at Shipley Art Gallery. Mrs Hetherington accompanied children.

12th September 1958 – Senior School
Mrs J.M. Nichols accompanied 47 girls to Dukes House Wood School in Hexham.

19th September: Girls returned to school.

September 1958
20 girls to Grammar School.
15 Technical College.
12 left 15 years old.

6 to Technical School.
12 to Beaconsfield School.

September 1959
10 girls to Grammar School
2 girls to Dame Allan's.
2 removed to other districts

6 to Secondary Technical School.
22 left 15 years old.

The School closed in July 1965. Pupils transferred to Greenwell Secondary Modern School.

Infants School

We played in the playground no matter what the weather. We had to go outside anyway because the toilets were at the top of the yard. The toilets were a scary place to be on your own if you asked to be excused during class to go. There was always the fear that the 'red hand' would get you or anyone else for that matter. Playing in the playground was such fun for school children. We chased each other around and played tag. We sat huddled in a corner talking about … I don't know. I never worried about being picked on as I was street wise and had an older brother in the next playground.

I also remember the little bottles of milk that each child was given to drink before morning playtime.

Junior and Senior School

At the age of seven going on eight I moved into the junior school. This was a rite of passage – I was growing up. The junior school was where my world became bigger. I was allowed to call for my friend Mary on my way to school. She and her family lived on Whitehall Road. Going back to school after dinner time I would call on another friend Mary who lived in Liddle Terrace. This was a street at the bottom of the senior yard and I would cut through to get to Mary's house. Also, friends called on me to go to school.

The teacher would send me on little messages to the head teacher or just to find out the time on the clock in the hall. I was so proud.

I was a big girl in junior school. Our Elizabeth, my younger sister was in the infants part of school. Moving up into junior and senior school was another rite of passage. I got more pocket money and was treated older. In senior school it was different because the boys and girls were separated and taught in a different section of the school.

Knotts on the High Street was where we sometimes went for shoes and school bags. They are also advertising 'Continental Type Jerseys styled by Matt Busby' – manager of Manchester United.

11 Plus Exam

At the end of junior school, children took an exam to determine which school they would go to after the age of eleven. This exam was called the 11 Plus. If a child passed the exam with good marks they might get a place at the boys or girls grammar school, or the technical school. If we didn't pass then we continued into the senior school or a secondary modern school education. The exam was taken about May/June time and the results came in a letter in July. I so desperately wanted to pass the 11 Plus and go to the Girls Grammar School on Dryden Road, Low Fell. My older sister had passed for the Technical School on Whitehall Road. Alas it wasn't meant to be and I continued post 11 at Brighton Avenue Senior School. I don't remember much about the senior school. I'd lost interest because I didn't pass the exam. At some point our Elizabeth came to the seniors and we were in the same class for a year. It was awful because if either of us got told off by the teacher the other child felt injured.

Gateshead's Grammar School for Girls.

Cookery/Sewing Classes

I learnt to cook at school. I learnt how to cook dinners, to bake cakes and become a future housewife. I also learned how to sew – another skill needed for a housewife and mother. To be honest I enjoyed it all. In sewing at the beginning of the school year I made an apron and hat of green gingham. These were to be worn during the cookery lesson. I also made a rag doll. As time went by, a skirt for myself which was such an achievement. I got to choose the material from a roll the teacher had in class. The material was blue striped. In between each stripe were little windmills and girls in clogs. I loved that skirt. It was gathered at the top with a waistband on it, quite a grownup skirt to me. I learnt how to do different types of stitching. There was also a treadle sewing machine to master. As well as these sewing skills I learnt how to iron. All needed for later life. Why did I need to go to grammar school? The boys did, they would get a job. That's why more of them passed the 11 Plus.

I enjoyed the things I did learn at school. A favourite of mine was knitting. Learning to knit began for me in the junior school when I made a pair of woollen mittens. I made them using four needles. Knitting the welt then continuing up a way until a place for the thumb was set by taking a few stitches from one of the needles using a big pin. The rest of the mitten was knitted to the top, then the thumb section was made. I did find the thumb tricky. I remember going to my Aunty Doreen's house in Saltwell Street just behind Rawling Road Methodist Church. Aunty Doreen showed me what to do and hey … two new mittens. I would attach the mittens at each end of a piece of the same coloured wool, then thread them down the sleeves of my coat. They hung out of the sleeves to be there for me in the cold weather during the autumn and winter months.

School Days Ended

Back then if a child didn't go to the grammar school they didn't take any GCE qualifications. This was a General Certificate of Education which helped towards getting a good job at 15 years of age. No grammar school for me therefore no certificate. I left school at fifteen unqualified. Never mind, my education had just begun. Within a few short months I took up night classes in shorthand, typing and English. This study happened three nights a week at Gateshead College on Durham Road at what was known as the top end of Saltwell Park. The college had been opened in 1955 by the Duke of Edinburgh.

Play

We were never allowed to play in the house. Well for a start it wasn't big enough and eventually with seven children under mam's feet it was not a good idea to be in the house.

'Go outside in the fresh air,' Mam would call. It didn't matter the weather, there was always something to do outside and someone to play with. The streets were full of children. I either played with one of my sisters or with a child from the street and it didn't matter whether boy or girl.

If it was raining, we played in the passage with our dolls imagining family things. We would tell our dolls stories while dressing and feeding them. It was all part of imaginary play. Our imagination was large. When the rain stopped we would run around in the street chasing each other. Following on from the doll play we would then take a doll for a walk in its pram. I can't recall having a pram to myself as we would share.

Once that game was over, we girls would say: 'Come on let's play two baller. This was throwing two balls against a wall, one after the other quite fast while chanting a song:

Dolls have always been popular toys with girls. Here nurses from Bensham Hospital in the 1930s have dolls for the little girls to play with.

'*Matthew ... Mark ... Luke and John ... Next door neighbour follow on.*' A girl standing beside me would catch one of the balls in her hand and continue to chant the ditty whilst throwing the balls against the wall. We each took turns and it was great fun. The game was not to let the balls drop on to the ground and to keep the rhythm going. The game would then change and one ball would be bounced off the ground and under a leg against the wall. We girls would tuck our dress into the legs of our knickers to make sure the ball didn't get caught in the hem line of our dress or skirt. This all happened chanting the little ditty.

Skipping was another favourite. I could skip on my own or join in with others. We would do ordinary skipping that involved three girls. There would be one girl at each end of the rope turning it while another would skip through the rope. While skipping, she would repeat at the same time a little song. We would take turns each to skip and hold the rope.

Then there was French skipping and this took a lot of skill. French skipping involved the two girls at either end holding a rope in each of their two hands and turning them at the same time. These ropes were old washing lines. They were long enough to be held and be slack enough when turned while a girl was skipping.

For French skipping the two ropes were turned together. Girls had to run into the moving ropes and jump up and down between the two ropes while chanting a song. It took a lot of practice to develop the skill of jumping between two ropes without getting tangled. Once tangled that was your turn finished and a change over with the rope holder. Everyone had a turn and others who were walking past would also join in.

Outside our flat, or our house as we called it, was a street lamp. In the early 1950s this lamp was a gas lamp that was lit up every evening by a gas man. He walked around the streets with a long pole and something on the end which he held up to the lamp and lit the mantle and it sprung into light. We girls and even boys made up games to play around the lamp.

Play was often centred around a gas lamp and here is one at the bottom of Bensham Avenue.

We would tie a skipping rope around it. At the other end, one of us girls would hold it while the other girl would skip or hop back and forward over it. The rope could be lifted higher and higher. When it became too high for jumping over, the game came to an end, or we changed from jumping to rope holding and the game started again. This was a competitive game to see who could jump the highest over the rope.

Another favourite game was 'hop scotch'. This game involved drawing a large square shaped box on the ground with chalk – someone always had chalk. The square became a house shape with a roof top. Then the square shape would be divided into 9 other squares within the larger square. In each of the squares the numbers 1 to 9 would be chalked in. The number 10 was chalked into the centre of the roof shape. To start, a stone would be thrown on to the number 1 square. The person would then, hopping on one leg, pick up the stone and throw it into the next numbered square, hop into that square and pick up the stone. On and on it went on to each of the other numbered squares until they reached the number 10. If the left or right foot went on the ground, it was game over.

We played with tops and whips. The whip leather at the end of a stick was wrapped around the stalk of the top. Then the top with the leather around it was thrown down on to the ground which released the top and it wound spin around. If the top looked to be slowing down I would whip it and it would spin fast again. As the top spun the actual top of it looked great if I had first coloured it with different coloured chalk. Chalks were generally pastel in colour thus the top would have pinks, blues and green on it. The colours looked good on the top as it spun around.

In later years, towards the end of the 1950s, the hula hoop craze began. It took lots of perseverance to learn this skill, spinning the hoop around my waist continuously without it falling to the ground. I was so pleased with myself when I succeeded.

Hide and seek was a great game outside because the hider could go into the back lanes and the church grounds to hide. It took a while to find those who were hiding. Also there was a statue of Jesus in a little recess just in the grounds of St Chad's Church (see page 14). The statue was on top of layered stones that looked like a

Playing out in Gateshead – My cousin Peter is on the trike with his friend, Terry Jones in the car.

seat … a throne. We would play Kings and Queens on it. We bairns never damaged anything in those days and we respected anything around a church.

We boys and girls became very street wise. With each other we would argue and call each other names and even hit each other. We learnt to stand up for ourselves. There was no going in to tell Mam what had happened with another girl or boy. If we did they would say: 'Telly tale tit … your tongue will be split' or 'no telling tales'. We would also say: 'Sticks and stones may break my bones, but names will never hurt me.'

If a girl had hit me and I went into the house crying, Mam would say: 'Go out and hit her back.' This way of doing things taught us to stand up for ourselves. My Mam never fought mine or anyone else's battles so we had to do it ourselves. She would never go and tell a parent what their child had done to her child. That was telling tales. She told me in later years that mams didn't do that because they knew that the children would be friends again very quickly, but it took a long time for the mams to make-up.

Back then we children had a lot of freedom to wander around. We learnt to look after ourselves. Communities were close and everyone knew everyone else. Parents kept an eye on other people's children and generally children were never alone. Not in our family, we always had a brother or sister with us.

Saltwell Park

As I got a bit older maybe eight or nine, I and others would go to Saltwell Park. This was either at weekends or in the school holidays. We would go into the park at the end of Brighton Road, near Ferndene Road. The first stop was the lake. Off came our shoes and socks and we sat on the ground with our feet dabbling in the water. We took our fishing nets to catch tiddlers and a jam jar with string around the top making a handle to hold and carry it. The tiddlers would then be put in to the jam jar which by now was filled with water from the lake. When the day was done we took the full jars home and they with the contents would be kept in the back yard. Unfortunately, the tiddlers would eventually die while any frogspawn turned into tadpoles and eventually frogs. This was a fascinating thing to watch. Once the tadpoles were frogs, we would let them out of the jars and watch them hop around on the ground.

Playing in Saltwell Park was even better than the local streets. We were well out of the view of the grown-ups or so we thought. If we were doing anything we should not be doing, we heard an adult call out: 'Mind I will tell your Mam.'

Also there was the Park attendant, or 'Parkee' as we called him, to watch out for us as well. Thus we were being watched all the time but we didn't realise.

I remember one particular fishing time. We, that's me and my sisters, would have been about nine or ten – I being the oldest of the three of us girls. Our new baby brother, born in November 1955 was still under one in the summer of 1956. We had pushed his pram with him in it to the park. Seeing a child pushing the pram around was a regular thing. I remember it was our Elizabeth who pushed the pram that day and she put the brake on the pram which was pointing towards the lake. Well we thought the brake was on ... but it wasn't and the pram rolled into the lake. There weren't any railings or barriers to stop it.

Our Elizabeth had to walk into the lake in her socks and shoes and was up to her knees in water. She pushed the pram out whilst I pulled it, using the handle, until it came out. Luckily, the water at this place where we fished wasn't very deep. Only the pram wheels got wet, unlike Elizabeth who had soaking wet shoes and socks and the hem of her dress. Never mind, it was summer and it wasn't long before she was dry. We never did tell mam because we would have been in trouble.

Strangely, no one ever told her ... I don't think? Mam was a wise woman and had eyes in the back of her head – as do all mams. She may have known but as we were safe nothing was said.

Here I am with my sister Elizabeth (left).

The boating lake on Saltwell Park has been popular for generations of Gateshead young 'uns.

Saltwell Park boating lake was an adventure. From a young age, and if we had money left from our pocket money, we would pay and go in a rowing boat. We pretended we were the Famous Five, even if there were only three of us. We took turns rowing the boat, which was difficult for young 'uns. No health and safety when we were young. On the other hand, we were aware that if we stood up in the boat it might tip over. When we changed places and took over the oars to row, we did it very carefully. There was a small island in the middle of the lake and the aim of the game was to row to it. We would get there, but never climbed out of the boat on to it. We knew it was a dangerous thing to do and anyway any attempts to do this were thwarted by the boat keeper blowing his whistle and gesturing as he shouted to us to get back in the boat.

Boat Landing, Saltwell Park, Gateshead, 10604

Two postcard views of the boating lake in Saltwell Park.

THE LAKE, SALTWELL PARK, GATESHEAD

If that lake could talk what a tale it would tell about our family. I remember our Allan had a green toy boat that looked like a yacht with white sails. He told me that one time when he was in the park sailing his little boat in the lake it went too far across. It got stuck against the little island in the middle. He was devastated and was very upset because he had to go home without it. 'Never mind son,' said Dad. 'I will get it back for you.'

That same night, when the park was all closed up, Dad went back. He climbed over the gates and, in the dark, walked to the lake. He took off his shoes and socks, rolled up his trousers and plodged across the lake to retrieve the boat. Allan was thrilled the next morning when he saw the boat on the kitchen table.

In Saltwell Park we would eat our jam sandwiches and drink our water which we took with us. The picnic was eaten while sitting on the grass near to the playground. We always kept back some of the bread to throw to the ducks and swans paddling about on the lake. In the playground there were swings, a very high slide and a roundabout – what we called a tea-pot lid because it looked like the lid of a tea-pot. There was also a monkey climb, which was a big metal climbing frame. We swung and climbed and slid down the slide. It was fun all day. To my knowledge as a child we never broke any bones jumping off the swing as it was going up high at speed, level with the bars at the top. No-one fell while climbing up the high metal stairs to wait at the top a turn to slide down the slide. We were street wise and knew our limitations because we were free to just get on with it.

Other adventures in the park revolved around the 'dene' – a wooded area which went down to a little stream. We played for hours making the trees into dens or even wigwams. We were the cowboys/girls or Indians/squaws and the den was the home.

We always had to visit the museum in the park. This housed exhibitions in glass cases of all kinds. There was a display cabinet with a model shop in it. The shop had little boxes and packets of tea, sugar, cocoa etc. There were counters with scales on them and little shop keeper models looking as if they were busy serving people.

The museum was on two floors. The shop was on the ground floor and also there were stuffed animals. I remember a stuffed fox and big stuffed birds which I found strange – didn't like them at all. There were statues of soldiers – fusiliers in red jackets. After looking at the shop and browsing the other things I would rush upstairs to look at the dolls house. This was an amazing sight for me. The dolls house I seem to remember stood on the floor in a glass display case. The front of the house was open to reveal three floors and stairs going to them. The ground floor was the usual sitting room, what I now know to be the drawing room, with a miniature grand piano in it and settees which looked more comfortable than ours at home. I was amazed at the standard floor lamp which I had never seen before. It was tall and the shade had tassels hanging down from it. There was also a kitchen on this floor. Upstairs there were bedrooms and these were not like the ones in our house. There were miniature four poster beds. There was also a wooden stand with a bowl and jug on it. In a corner there was a little chair upholstered in what looked like velvet. There was a child's room with a wooden cradle on the floor and wooden toys all around. Also there were dolls of all shapes and sizes in the little rooms. I stood looking at it for a long time.

When we got bored with the museum we would make our way back through the park to the main gate. On the way back we played kings and queens in the turrets around the tower. We eventually arrived at pets corner where there were cages with animals in them. The animals weren't necessarily pets but animals none the less. There was a selection of budgerigars in cages. In a circular cage there were peacocks showing off their multi-coloured feathers displaying a beautiful feather span. There were rabbits and guinea pigs while in another round cage there were other small animals I did not know the names of.

We skipped, jumped and ran until we reached the Rose Garden. More imaginary play took place in here. Usually family play because in the garden there were seats with roses growing around them and over them making them look like little houses with a roof and walls. We imagined each of these seats as a little house and played houses in them.

In the Rose Garden I and my sisters would pick up the rose petals which had fallen onto the grass. We took them home and made perfume from them. This was done by putting them in a jar, adding water and leaving the contents to settle. A few days later the water was the perfume. We were never bored at least I never was. We stayed in the park all day having fun. But we were always back in time for tea.

Saltwell Park House, Gateshead

Saltwell Park House which we visited to see the fascinating museum inside. The park is still a great place to visit today.

Saltwell Park had wonderful places for us to play in.

Winter Play

The dark winter nights didn't stop us from playing outside. Even when it snowed the street was packed with children sledging. We would start at the top of our street and sledged all the way down to the bottom. This was all on the road but no cars came down our cobbled street. Dragging my sledge, I would walk back up to the top of our bit of the street and start again. Older boys would start at the top of Westminster Street on Rectory Road and sledge down the entire street until their sledge would stop.

One winter snowy night, walking back up the street, dragging my sledge behind me, a child sledging down the street bumped into me knocking me to the ground. I fell flat onto my face and there was blood everywhere. Someone went for Mam and an ambulance was rung – a rare thing in those days. I think I was taken to the Children's Hospital or it might have been the Queen Elizabeth. My face was x-rayed and luckily nothing broken. However, I had a very big swollen nose now and my eyes and cheeks were puffy. I didn't go to school for a few weeks which I thought was great. I would be about nine or ten.

There was a little ditty we children would chant when we saw an ambulance coming along the road:

There weren't many cars on the road where we lived but there were still warnings such as this printed in the Gateshead Post.

> *Touch your collar*
> *Never follow*
> *Never get the fever.*
> *Touch your toes*
> *Touch your nose*
> *Never go in one of those.*

So I was very scared to be in an ambulance (like the one below) going to the hospital that night.

When I got roller skates for Christmas one year, a friend and I would skate outside of the grocery shop. The shop keeper left the shop lights on overnight. We girls would pretend we were ice skaters at the ice rink and the light was our spot light. I was about 10 nearly 11 at this point. I got these ideas from the Bunty comic for girls which was first published in 1958. It was aimed at the under 14 age group. There was also a Bunty Annual which I received as a gift for Christmas. Inside the mag and book were little comic strips of girls who were ice skaters, horse riders or ballet dancers. The nearest I could come was to be an ice skater.

My childhood days were such fun in Westminster Street and the larger community.

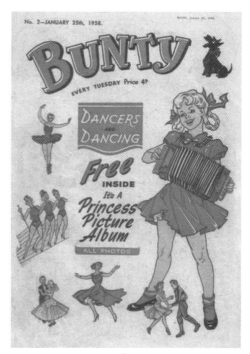

A Bunty comic that was very popular for girls and gave us some ideas for our play. The annuals were also a favourite present at Christmas.

Entertainment

Made up plays

In the 1950s we made our own entertainment. My sisters and I would put on little plays which took place in the backyard. There would be plenty of Mam's clothes to dress up in, coats, skirts, shoes, scarves, pinnies etc, and we would write something down on paper with each child having a part to play. Sometimes we would act out life … looking after the baby using a doll … going to school … being in class … and all that school involved. This acting was our way of incorporating experiences of life into ourselves.

Palladium

I looked forward to going to the 'flicks' as we called the pictures on a Saturday afternoon. It was off to the matinee at the Palladium (known as the Pal) on Saltwell Road. One of the pictures which we saw was usually a serial called 'Flash Gordon' which was the science fiction of the day and very futuristic – somewhere in the 21st century or beyond. There was always a princess to be rescued … which I enacted all the following week.

There were also the Cowboy and Indian films and, when we came out of the pictures, we then chased after each other with

The Palladium (known as the Pal) on Saltwell Road.

imaginary guns, bows and arrows. I loved being a cowgirl or even the Indian girl who had been captured by the cowboys and had to be rescued by the Indians. The action and our imagination got us home.

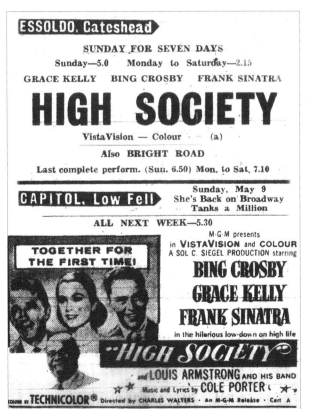

High Society was on at the Essoldo and Capitol, Low Fell.

Other films I loved featured 'The Three Stooges'. These were three men doing idiotic things to get a laugh, which was such fun. There was always 'Pathe News' which showed us what was happening in the country (perhaps the Queen's Coronation) as well as news from the rest of the world.

Coatsworth

When I was older, maybe ten or eleven, I would go to the Coatsworth pictures. This cinema was just off Coatsworth Road and the grown up place to be. I would go on a Wednesday afternoon in the school holidays. Mr Stephenson the greengrocer, would give us the tickets. Shop owners were given complimentary tickets from the cinema to be used on Wednesdays afternoon because shops back then were closed. The kind Stephensons gave their tickets, if they didn't want to use them, to Mam or maybe another family in the street, taking turns to share them.

I really enjoyed the films in the 1950s. It was the Doris Day era and she was in 'By the Light of the Silvery Moon' with Gordon MacRae and 'Pillow Talk' with Rock Hudson.

Other films I enjoyed included: 'Carousel', 'Singing in the Rain', 'High Society' and 'Roman Holiday'.

I loved the fashion portrayed in these films: the straight skirts and little jackets. I would copy the look for my doll and I sat for hours making the little doll sized clothes by hand. Other films during this era were Walt Disney films such as 'Snow White', 'Cinderella' and 'Sleeping Beauty'.

The other films I saw, thinking about it now, would have been for older people. I saw them, though how I got in is beyond me. There were different rated films in those days: 'U' (for everyone, normally children, 'A' (slightly older films and you had to be accompanied by an adult) and 'X' rated (adults only). I was never allowed in for X rated films.

At the end of the 1950s there was Elvis Presley in 'Jail House Rock' and I wasn't allowed to go to see this. This was the Teddy Boy era and not for children.

Cinema performances

The Coatsworth would open about 1 o'clock showing films from then until 10 o'clock at night – they just rolled on and on. People and us bairns might go into the pictures in the middle of the films and stay well into the next session until we had caught up with what we had missed. Between each performance, we children, if unaccompanied would go into the toilets until the lights went out, ready waiting for the next show. We would then sneak back in, sit in a different seat and watch again. The usherettes must have seen us, but no one threw us out. We could stay there for hours – bairns had such freedom back then.

Carousel, one of my favourite films, was shown at the Bensham Picture House.

Above: An advert for the Coatsworth Cinema, including 'The Flame and the Flesh' that was 'Cert. 'X' – Adults only'.

Left: The popular Gateshead cinema, the Odeon on the High Street, seen here around 1950.

Radio

The radio was very much family entertainment. On Saturday mornings there was 'Children's Favourites'. This was a programme with songs such as 'How much is that doggy in the window?', 'Torchy, the battery boy', 'I'm a pink toothbrush, you're a blue toothbrush' and others I have forgotten.

A popular programme during the week was 'Housewives Choice' for mams to listen to. On Sunday it was 'Two Way Family Favourites' for the whole family to listen to during Sunday roast dinner time. The men abroad in the forces and their families at home would request songs for each other over the radio. This programme was followed with my Dad's favourite 'The Billy Cotton Band Show'. Billy was a band conductor of the day and with his band of all sorts of musicians and singers would entertain the listeners for an hour.

There was also 'Meet The Huggetts', a family comedy with Kathleen Harrison and Jack Warner who was famous on television in 'Dixon of Dock Green'. Another comedy was 'Around the Horne' with Kenneth Horne and there was 'The Goons' with Spike Milligan, Harry Secombe, Michael Bentine and Peter Sellers. We enjoyed 'Educating Archie' with ventriloquist Peter Brough and Archie Andrews his doll. We were also allowed to listen to the 'Paul Temple' detective mystery stories.

A wireless could be bought at R. Johnston's shops on West Street and Coatsworth Road.

Dad was very good with building his own radios and we had one in our bedroom, which he let us listen to when we went to bed. I think this was on the nights Mam was at work at Mr and Mrs Bowmaker's fried fish shop up the Avenues or at a Whist Drive at St Chad's.

Piano/accordion

Dad was very musical and he played either a piano accordion or the piano. The piano eventually replaced the cot in the corner of the kitchen. Later there was a ukulele that Dad loved to play as he sang 'I'm leaning on the lamp-post at the corner of the street'. We would sometimes invite the neighbourhood kids into our house and have a sing song.

Home Movies

At home there was other entertainment, such as Dad doing a film show. This involved him hanging a white sheet from the picture rail against the wall. Then he would bring out a film projector and a reel of film would be placed on the side of the projector. The film would roll and the images would appear on the sheet on the wall. There wasn't any sound but it was fun watching Mickey Mouse and Tom & Jerry. We never did find out where he got all this from. Sometimes kids from the street came in to watch whatever film it was that night. We were never bored living in Westminster Street.

An advert from 1952 to buy a piano from Geo. Wilkes & Son – 'No Deposit! 1 month's approval! 10 /- weekly'.

Television

During this period of time Rediffusion was installed in our street. This was a series of cables placed underground with a cable going into the home. We didn't have a television in our home but some families in Westminster Street did.

Upstairs, before my Aunt and Uncle moved in, lived a family that did have a television and I loved going upstairs to watch 'The Railway Children'. Children's programmes started at 5 o'clock every evening with very little on before that except the 'test card' – a still image of a little girl, with a hairband in her long hair, at a blackboard.

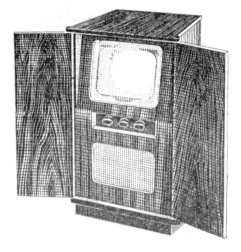

A free seven day television trial was on offer some time in the 1950s. Each family in the street, us included, took turns in having a free trial for the week consecutively. It was great fun going in and out of each other's homes to watch the TV. The only channel was the BBC. Other ways to watch television was to go down the High Street and watch it through the television shop window.

Right: A cabinet style television from the 1950s.

Dancing

Our Elizabeth when she was young went to 'Victor Silvester's Dance' at the Odeon Studio on the High Street in Gateshead. Elizabeth recalls: 'It was part of the Odeon Cinema. I went in through a door at the side of the main entrance to the pictures. It was upstairs to a big hall. I remember huge windows across one wall. Mind when you are young everything is huge. I learnt Ballroom Dancing there including the dances of the time, such as waltzes and foxtrots.'

She also went to the Little Theatre near Saltwell Park. This was an outing organised by Brighton Avenue School. Our Allan can also remember going to the Little Theatre.

Our Allan was a Morris Dancer and learnt that through school. A group of boys would dance outside St Chad's Church on a Saturday morning.

'Learn to Dance the Victor Silvester Way' at the Odeon Theatre, Gateshead. A junior club gave dance tuition for 8 to 15 year olds.

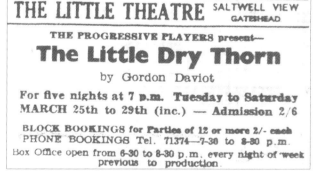

An advert for a production at the Little Theatre, Saltwell View.

The Hoppings

The Hoppings are a yearly fair held on Newcastle's Town Moor. It was great fun and I went for years with Dad along with a brother or sister. My favourite rides were the dodgem cars, the helter-skelter, the carousel and the side shows. Dad would throw a ball to knock down a coconut and if he succeeded we got the coconut to take home. Then there was the Candy Floss that was pink and gooey and seemed to took ages to eat it. But by the time we walked back home from the moor, down through Newcastle and over the High Level Bridge it was eaten.

Food

Food was rationed at the start of the Second World War and lasted until 1954. Therefore at the beginning of the 1950s food was scarce with some items still rationed. Sweets for example were a rarity until the end of rationing.

Mam, however, always provided a meal or something on the table for us to eat.

Breakfast

Breakfast was always porridge. My younger sister said: 'Do you not remember our Kath? It was served up on a plate as thick as bulls' lugs.'

It did bring back memories. The porridge was the shape of the round tea plate, more like a pancake than porridge.

The milk was delivered fresh every morning, in glass bottles, on to our front door step. We, that's each child, would fight to get to the milk bottle with cream on top of the milk. We would share the little bit of cream between us and, with a sprinkle of sugar, it was delicious.

If we wanted more to eat after the porridge it would have been jam and bread and generally with a cup of tea to drink.

Sunday Breakfast was special. It would be some version of bacon, eggs and tinned tomatoes. This would be on the plate or made into sandwiches with stottie cake. A cup of tea to go with it always tasted good very good, don't know why?

A pint and half pint milk bottles. On the pint bottle it says 'Please rinse and return' with the following rhyme:

'On each new day your milkman collects bottles by the score. But what will please him most of all YOUR empties by the door.'

Dinner Time

Lunch, or dinner time as it was called, was around twelve noon. My siblings and I came home from school for dinner. Some children received a free school meal at dinner time which was always a cooked meal. This would consist of meat, potatoes and vegetables – usually carrots and turnip in the winter, and carrots and cabbage in the summer with other added vegetables when in season. Back then people ate locally produced vegetables. My Uncle Sid had an allotment near Saltwell Cemetery on Saltwell Road, opposite the Park, and we got vegetables from him. Nothing or very little at this stage was imported on the scale it is today.

On a Sunday there was roast meat, mashed potatoes, vegetables and a Yorkshire pudding. This was always followed by a milk pudding – whole rice, ground rice, Semolina, Sago or Tapioca. These puddings could be made and shared a long way around a big family.

Another pudding I remember was spotty dick. This was a homemade steam pudding made from flour, suet and dates mixed with water. The mixture was placed in a pudding dish then greaseproof paper was placed over it and kept in place by tying string around it. The pudding dish was placed in a steamer over hot water and cooked for a very long time.

During the week the meals were predictable:

Monday dinner was left over roast from Sunday, which was always a roast of beef, lamb or pork. We never had chicken in those days.

Tuesday was minced beef and dumplings with potatoes and vegetables, including peas when in season.

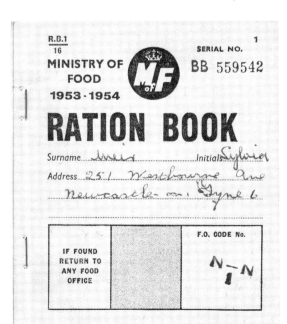

A ration book from 1953-54 – the last year of rationing.

Wednesday was liver and onions with the usual vegetables.

Thursday was homemade oven baked steak and kidney pie.

On Friday it was homemade fish and chips. This would have been fried in a chip pan on the top of the stove or fish cakes, also homemade. There was sometimes 'roll mops' which was herring rolled up and a skewer put through to hold the fish in place, then it was baked in the oven. I liked it with vinegar on it, but not a popular choice for others.

On Saturday I have a vague memory of this but my older brother Allan recalls: 'I think we had bacon and egg, or meat squares, corned beef pie or corned beef hash.'

I liked all of the food put before me, which was lucky because if it didn't get eaten at dinner time it had to be eaten at tea time. Another food I liked was tripe and onions even though I wasn't sure what meat it was at the time but it was tasty. My brother hated some of the food presented to him and he was once in trouble for putting some sort of stew in the pocket of his school jacket and on his way to school he threw it away. This was a very naughty thing to do as food was a scarcity. Not eating it, or putting it in a school jacket pocket and throwing it away outside was not a good thing to do. It's funny now, but not back then.

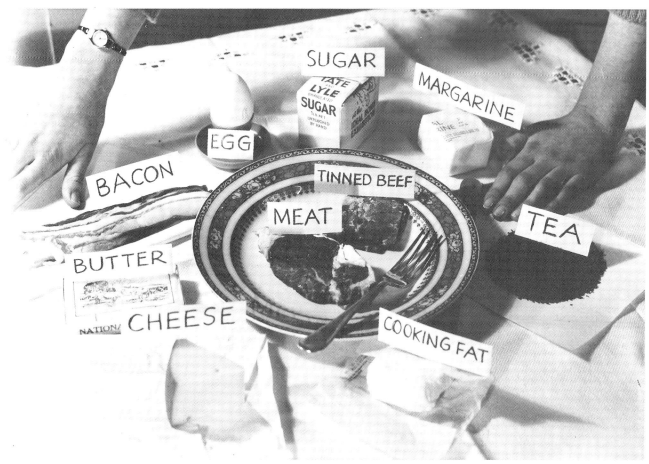

The weekly portions of food for a person during rationing. Note one egg per person a week!

Tea Time

Tea was around 4 o'clock after school and was generally sandwiches made from sardines, spam, bananas when available and some sort of paste or spread from a little jar of different flavours. I think the product name was Shippam. There would also be homemade cake or biscuits. Sugar was rationed and it went further if in cakes etc. Any baked food left over from weekend meals was eaten up during the weekly meals.

Sunday tea was special as there was plenty of food because Mam baked all day on a Saturday. We had cakes, scones and biscuits. There were also pies – either savoury meat or sweet fruit. We rarely got fresh fruit to hold in our hands to eat and if we did it was an apple cut into four portions with each child getting a quarter. Two apples went a long way in our house. There was always a trifle made with jelly, custard, cream and sometimes in the bottom of the trifle would be fruit salad out of a tin.

Snacks and Supper

If we were hungry between meals during the day we were allowed bread and butter and a drink of water. The bread and butter were just 'lush' and sometimes we could spread sweet condensed milk on it, or sprinkle sugar onto it. There was also a spread called 'drippin' made from the juices of the Sunday roast. The juices and the fat were left to go cold and thick, then it could be spread on bread. Another treat on occasions was bread toasted over the fire in the evenings. The slice of bread would be placed on the end of a long wooden-handled, three prong fork and held over the fire until it was toasted golden brown. I would spread the toast with butter and it would melt into the bread. Sometimes I would spread the toast with golden syrup. I can still conjure up the taste and smell.

I loved those cosy dark winter evenings around the kitchen fire. There was the sound of crackling coals and the smell of smoke produced from the red hot burning coals. The fire would light up the kitchen and the hot buttered toast was so delicious. I have fond memories of Westminster Street.

Here are some adverts for local food producers.

Below are two bakers – Hunters and Hendees.

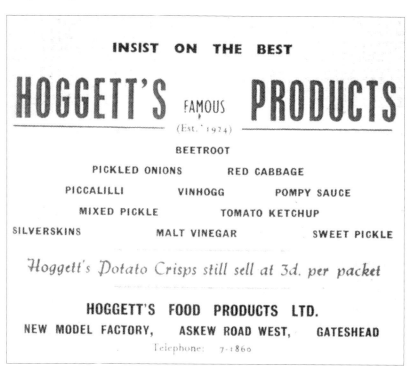

An advert for local food producer Hoggett's of Askew Road West. They were established in 1924 and this list of products from 1959 includes such favourites as pickled onions, tomato ketchup, piccalilli and sweet pickle. They were also selling potato crisps at 3d per packet.

An advert for Powells of Low Fell. They were known for their jams, marmalade and sauces.

High Days and Holidays

New Year ... New Beginnings

New Year's Eve ended the old year and New Year's Day began the new one. New Year's Eve was special in our house. Mam would lay a new table cloth on the table and place Christmas cake, mince pies, a bottle of Sherry, and Sherry Glasses on to the table.

'Why do you do that?' I asked when young.

'It's for the first footers,' she would reply.

'What are they?' I continued.

'At 12 midnight, when Big Ben in London chimes the time on the radio, the old year is gone and the New Year begins.'

I hadn't any idea what she meant but knew it was important. 'What's a first footer?' I asked again.

'It's the first person to put their foot across the front step and come through the front door and into the house.'

'Yes,' I kept on, 'but why is this special?'

Mam would sigh at all these questions but I kept on and on till I got an answer I could understand. 'The first footer brings with them a piece of coal, to keep the fire going. This will keep the house warm through the year. A piece of cake to make sure we don't go hungry. Also a pocket full of money which will make sure we have money. All these things are to bring us luck throughout the New Year. Now go to bed.'

She must have been asked these questions a million times. I wanted to stay up and see this wonder but she never would let me.

I had lots of questions when I was young.

Lent to Easter

February saw the beginning of Lent. Pancake Tuesday was the day before Lent officially started and usually people gave up something they liked or fasted for the six weeks of Lent until Easter. It was traditionally eggs a lot of people give up, thus, Pancake Day was celebrated. Mam made pancakes for us all at dinner time. We would have our usual Tuesday dinner of mince and dumplings followed with a pancake covered with golden syrup or with sugar sprinkled on it and a squirt of lemon over it all. Having pancakes would use up the eggs and there would be no more until Easter Sunday.

The next day was the religious day of Ash Wednesday. Strangely I remember as a child I quite enjoyed this day as in our school, children were allowed to go to a morning service at their church. A few of us girls would go to the church on Bensham Road, I think St Cuthbert's. We were allowed to take part in the morning service and sometimes we would be brave enough to go forward to receive the communion and have the sign of the cross placed on our forehead in ash. When the service was over, we walked back to school along Brighton Road and this meant we were late to school – around 10 to 10.30ish. You bet we made the trip out last as long as we could. It was all legal and above board but I never told Mam. We were Methodists and went to church and Sunday school at the Methodist Church on the corner of Rawling Road and Whitehall Road. Our Allan said the church was known locally as 'The Trinity'.

The beginning of Lent was usually the beginning of spring. Mam would give us a tablespoon full of spring medicine which was a homemade concoction of I think lemon juice and not sure what else. It tasted good so felt it would do me good. To me it wasn't any different from taking cod liver oil from a spoon that was given to me and my brother and sisters most days.

An advert for Cod Liver Oil. Mam also gave us a dose of her 'spring medicine'.

Lent and the following six Sundays until Easter Sunday were special times for me. In our house each Sunday was remembered by chanting a little ditty: *'Tid, Mid, Miseray, Carlin, Palm and Paste Egg Day.'* Not sure what these terms meant as a child. The ones that have stayed with me are 'Miseray' because I always said 'Misery' and thought because of Good Friday that was what it was. Carlin Sunday was because with Sunday roast there would be Carlin peas. Palm Sunday followed. During the Palm Sunday church service, or Sunday school, each child was given a piece of Palm in the shape of a cross. The last Sunday of Lent was Easter Sunday. We children would have painted hard boiled eggs known as paste eggs. These were the eggs we got on Easter Sunday … but not to be eaten. The following day, Easter Monday, was when the eggs got eaten.

The whole family would go to Saltwell Park. Mam made a picnic of sandwiches and cakes. There were a lot of families in the park on that special day. Everyone sat on the wide grass space just beside the Pavilion going down towards the boating lake. Somewhere in the day we children and lots of others would roll our beautifully coloured and painted paste eggs down the grass towards the lake. The egg shells would obviously crack and when the race was over we could eat a whole egg. It was such fun. I remember the day with such happy memories of Easter and Saltwell Park.

Saltwell Park is where many Gateshead people have had very happy days.

Birthday Parties

Generally during Lent it would be my birthday. In March it was also two of my cousins' birthdays and we were all the same age. One birthday, 7th March for our Janice, who lived near the park. Another birthday was the 14th March for my cousin Tommy Jones, born on Rectory Road at my Gran's house, but eventually lived in Birmingham. And my birthday was 28th March. There were a lot of signposts to my birthday and the end of Lent. Each year this was all a special time for me.

Neither I, nor my sisters or brothers ever had a birthday party. There were already too many children in our house, and because of rationing not enough food. I did go to other people's birthday parties. One family, called Wass, who lived the next flat down, had parties. There was Stephen, Malcolm and Pamela and for each of their birthdays there would be a party. I really enjoyed going along. In particular because there was good food and not that much different to what we got at home on a Sunday. However, inside one of the scones there was money – a sixpence wrapped in grease proof paper. I would sit, as would others, reaching for a scone in the hope I would be the lucky one. I don't think I was.

There were always party games to play: musical chairs; pass the parcel; pin the tail on the donkey; blind man's bluff; and I am sure I won one of these games and got a prize.

Empire Day

Apart from the summer school holidays and the half term holidays, most holidays were a religious holidays. In addition there was also Empire Day. Every year, in May for a few years in the early 1950s we celebrated this day.

'Of course there was a little chant to remember,' said our Allan. 'It was simply – *Empire Day, 24th of May*'.

School began with an Empire Day assembly. We did lessons around topics of the Empire of Great Britain that included Canada, Australia, India and parts of Africa. We were taught about each country and its climate, flowers and animals. We knew that in Canada there was the Maple tree, the Mounted Police and Niagara Falls. In Australia there were the Kangaroos, the Koala Bears and the Kookaburra birds. There was also Tasmania, an island, just off Australia. Africa had poor black children and every year we could buy a little picture of one of them and the money went to help them in some way. I loved my little picture of a black faced girl with tight curls or pigtails in her hair.

We would sing hymns such as 'Jerusalem' as well as 'God Save the Queen' before we could go home for the afternoon. We learnt a lot about the world through Empire Day.

Children celebrating Empire Day with Gateshead's Mayor in the 1930s.

The Coronation

In February 1952 Queen Elizabeth II came to the throne. The following year in June there seemed to be a Coronation street party in every part of Gateshead. Each mother baked and prepared food for the family. It was then brought out and placed on one of the long tables stretching from the bottom to the top of our street. The street was shrouded with union flag bunting. I think we each got a Coronation cup with a picture of the new Queen on it. It was a lovely day and I remember I got so excited about it all and became ill. Mam had to take me into the house for a rest … I was only five years old.

Left: An advert for Coronation beakers given out to children under five years of age in Gateshead in May 1953. It seems very well organised and to receive a beaker 'the ration book (green) for each child must be produced'.

COUNTY BOROUGH OF GATESHEAD

Coronation of H.M. Queen Elizabeth II.
Distribution of Beakers

BEAKERS for children UNDER 5 YEARS OF AGE resident in Gateshead will be distributed as follows:—

WEDNESDAY, 27th MAY

Distribution Centre	Time	Children with Surnames commencing with letters:
TOWN HALL:	9-30 a.m. — 12 noon	A — E
	1-30 p.m. — 4-30 p.m.	F — L
MINERS HALL. WREKENTON:	9-30 a.m. — 12 noon	All letters
RAVENSWORTH METHODIST CHURCH. BEECHWOOD GARDENS:	9-30 a.m. — 12 noon	All letters

THURSDAY, 28th MAY

TOWN HALL:	9-30 a.m. — 12 noon	M — R
	1-30 p.m. — 4-30 p.m.	S — Z

THE RATION BOOK (GREEN) for each child MUST be produced. Children should NOT be brought to the place of distribution.

Town Hall,
GATESHEAD, 8.
20th May, 1953.

J. W. PORTER,
Town Clerk.

Whit Monday

The next holiday of the year was in May or June which was the Whitsun church holiday. There was always a trip to the seaside on what was called Whit Monday and it was the yearly Methodist Sunday School trip. There was always a bus to take children, mams and dads and other family members away for the day. It didn't matter the weather – off we went. I remember such fun and excitement as we travelled and sang on our way to Tynemouth.

Beaches were full of people back then. Mam would find a good spot and each child would put down the bag they were carrying or a bucket and spade. If the weather was good off came the clothes, no swimming costumes, no t-shirts, only navy knickers. I would rush down to the water's edge to plodge in the sea. As time went by, and I could swim a bit, Dad taught me how to swim in the sea.

A packed Tynemouth Long Sands – a popular destination for Gateshead families on Whit Monday.

I have a couple of vivid memories of these trips out. One time I got lost when I might have been seven or eight years old – I think at the water's edge when I began moving along the coast line. When I finished plodging and playing I turned around to go back up the beach to my family but I couldn't see where they were. I walked up the beach to where I thought they were but couldn't find them and began to cry. A lady realised I was lost and took me to what I thought was the place where the grown-ups could get hot water to make a cup of tea. The attendant asked my name and announced over the loud speaker that there was a lost girl. Mam came to collect me with much relief for the both of us – but at the same time I got told off for getting lost.

Another time it rained non-stop. We all came off the beach and stood in the archways of the houses on the front street. We sheltered here from the rain until the bus came back for us – it was a long time. A lady came out of her house and invited us all in for shelter and a cup of tea.

Another fond memory is about the sandwiches on seaside days. They were always egg and, no matter how hard I tried as a child, I would always drop mine on to the sandy beach.

'Rub it off,' Mam would say. Food was never thrown away.

I did try to rub the sand off. For me as a child the sand became part of the sandwich. If all of the sand didn't rub off, it became egg and sand sandwiches.

Days Out

The big summer holidays from school were great. We as a family didn't always go away on holiday but Mam and Dad would take a few of us on day trips. Not away to far-off places but a long walk to the country. The countryside was a walk down to the Team Valley along to Lamesley past Ravensworth Castle and up to Sunniside or Kibblesworth. For us children in the 1950s these were far-off places. There was always a picnic of sorts with plenty bottles of water from the tap which we drank on a stretch of green grass at the road side. We bairns took turns riding up high on Dad's shoulders and we used our imagination to play our new country games. It was all very exciting.

Ryton Willows

One summer school holiday in 1952 Mam and Dad took us all on a camping holiday for two weeks to Ryton Willows, a place to go by the River Tyne. At this point there were six children in the family. There was a lot of stuff needed to camp – two tents, primus stove, all the food and other things needed for six young children. We travelled there in the van belonging to our milk man. He drove us and our stuff to the Willows and helped us unload on to a good spot, then he went home. We camped out for two weeks. Dad put up the tents tying them together with the string from each of the entrances. One tent was a large one in which you could stand up and served as a bedroom for Mam, Dad and baby. The other was a smaller one where the five other children slept. Or it might have been the other way around. We all slept in the tent with blankets on the ground to lie on and blankets over us. It was the summer so not cold.

Dad cooked breakfast on a little stove. Porridge through the week and bacon sandwiches on Sunday. Mam would cook some sort of meal at dinner time while we children would play all day. We would go down to the river and plodge a bit, then use our imagination to make up games and explore the new area we found ourselves in.

One evening, with my elder sister and brother, we walked across the fields and over a little bridge to the Newburn pictures. It was a scary film and I was terrified walking back across the field in the dark.

The milkman was to come and take us home at the end of two weeks but he never showed up. Dad went on to the main road and asked a driver passing by if he would take us all home. I am happy to say he obliged. What an adventure!

Evening Chronicle Sunshine Fund

Another holiday I remember was when I and one of my sisters went away to Scotland with the 'Evening Chronicle Sunshine Fund'. The day came and Mam took us to Gateshead's Town Hall. Other children and mams were there as well as back then it was usually the mams who looked after the children. The dads were generally at work. There was a big coach with comfortable seats to take us to Scotland. On the way we sang songs on the journey and generally enjoyed the trip.

We stayed in dormitories and slept in bunk beds. Mam gave me a little toilet bag and inside were a face cloth and soap, toothbrush and paste to share between us. I was the eldest so I had to look after the bag and my sister. Each morning we went to the place where there were sinks to wash, then back to the dormitory to dress and go to another dormitory to have breakfast.

I remember we went to Holyrood Palace for the day. It was a palace and thus began my love of stately homes. Picnics of jam and other sandwiches also became a favourite of mine.

Right: The Sunshine Fund featured in the Evening Chronicle.

SUNSHINE FUND CAMP WAS GREAT SUCCESS

ONE hundred children have returned to their homes on Tyneside after having had a wonderful time at the Chronicle Sunshine Fund's holiday camp at Meigle, Perthshire.

Many of the children held bunches of heather as they left the motor coaches that had brought them from Scotland.

Mrs. E. Blyth, W.V.S. children's specialist who was in charge of the party, said of the holiday: "It was a success despite bad weather in the latter half of the week."

Concerts, film shows

She said the children soon settled down and enjoyed the amenities of the camp—the good food, the concerts and film shows and the outside sports.

Mrs. Blyth added: "We have seen the colour come back into their cheeks and have seen the shy children respond and mix with the other members of the party.

"We have had a wonderful time and the workers have worked extremely hard."

Dukes House Wood School Camp

I think in September 1958, when I was in the senior school, a lot of children in our class and other classes went on holiday to Dukes House Wood Camp, near Hexham, for two weeks. It was great because we didn't have to go to proper school for a while. I think it cost Mam £1 for the two weeks which was a lot of money in those days. We shared the girls' dormitories, with bunk beds to sleep in. We ate cornflakes for breakfast, a treat for me and as many jam sandwiches as we liked.

Gateshead youngsters at Dukes House Wood School Camp.

There were film nights at the camp and I remember one film 'Elephant Walk' with Elizabeth Taylor. It was obviously about elephants in Africa and how they were killed because they walked through a man's house built on an old elephant trail.

I got to take up photography. Not only did I take the photograph but I and others got to develop it from a negative to a picture, using all kinds of chemicals in trays for the processing and developing.

I met other girls from a school in Middlesbrough. Good friends were made in the time I was there.

Our class, maybe more than one class, walked into Hexham on the Sunday morning to visit the Abbey, then walk back again. I remember it was fun going down the bank into Hexham with my friends. It was not fun going back to camp as it was a very steep bank. On the Sunday, mams could visit us for the day bringing little goodies.

Another time we walked along the Roman Wall and I remember it poured with rain. It was still fun and even better eating our sandwiches along the way.

Right: A movie poster for Elephant Walk.

Sunday School Anniversary

Sometime during the summer months there was the Rawling Road Methodist Church Sunday School Anniversary. This was another special time. Each year all Sunday School children had to take part in a concert to celebrate their past year at Sunday School. Children would sit in rows across the stage while parents and adults sat in the audience. We, that's my two younger sisters, each 15 months younger than the other, always sat together. We got new dresses with new shoes and socks for this occasion. I remember one year my sisters and I all had the same patterned spotty dress on but in different colours – red and white, blue and white and turquoise and white. We all had black patent leather shoes with a strap across the foot and fastened with a buckle and new white socks. Each child had a verse or a line to learn. We would have practised for a couple of weeks. Not to worry, when it was my turn to speak out my little verse I would watch Mam. She would sit in the audience and mouth the verse for me to see. I never forgot the verse on any of these occasions. At the end of the concert each child was given a religious book as a prize. Just inside the cover would be your name and the year of the anniversary. We could take the book home. I was so very proud.

A book given as a prize at a Sunday School Anniversary.

The Methodist Church on Rawling Road where we went to Sunday School.

Harvest Festival

In September it would be the church Harvest Festival. Hymns on this occasion that we sang were 'We plough the fields and scatter the good seed on the land' and 'All things bright and beautiful'. Myself and others would take an item of food to church. During the service, each pew of children in turn took their food item to the front of the church and placed it on a table. When the service was over a group of children with an adult would walk to the local hospital and deliver the food.

Right: A collection of food and decorations for Harvest Festival.

Bonfire Night

Guy Fawkes Night on the 5th November was the next highlight. To us it was 'bonfire night'. We would spend weeks getting ready to build a street bonfire. We also made a guy that was a stuffed man made out of old clothes with usually trousers tied at the ankles to make sure the stuffing of newspaper didn't fall out. The top of the man was made up of a jacket with again sleeves tied at the wrists to keep the stuffing in. The head was made from papier-mache and painted. Anyone who wanted to join in would go around the streets pulling the guy sitting on a bogy that Allan had made from planks of wood and old pram wheels. We would ask the grown-ups for a 'penny for the guy'. We were given money which we used to buy fireworks – bangers, catherine wheels, sparklers and rockets. We would also collect wood and other items that were discarded which would be placed on the road in the middle of the street. This became by bonfire night a very big pile of stuff to be lit. It was the older boys who would set it

My brother Allan.

alight and also set off the fireworks and hand out the sparklers to the younger children. I also remember as a child throwing big potatoes into the edge of the fire. They were left to bake then I would drag it out with a stick. These potatoes were very tasty.

Christmas

Then it would be the Christmas season. There were a lot of parties to go to. At school each child took to school a dish and a spoon. They had to have coloured wool wrapped around the spoon and the bottom of the dish would have my name written on it. This was to identify each child's items to be used for the custard and jelly we were given at the party. I was always terrified I didn't get my own things back. In the run up to Christmas, we made the decorations to go up in school. They were generally paper chains and we were allowed to decorate the classroom with them. I don't remember a Christmas tree, just paper chains. The school hall was decorated ready for the party games. There were games of musical chairs as well as Scottish country dancing.

There were the Sunday School parties. One at the Methodist Church Hall which was on the corner of Whitehall Road and Coatsworth Road. At some point there were the Girls Guide parties in the Presbyterian Church Hall. This church was on the corner of Whitehall Road and Brighton Road opposite Brighton Avenue School.

I went to other Christmas parties such as the Odeon Cinema party on the High Street (see page 26). To me a small child, the Odeon was a wonderful awesome building – very regal with an ornate entrance hall way with ornamental carving on the walls. The door into the stalls was a double door, small in size and dark in colour. The seats inside were soft cushioned red and so very comfortable. At the Christmas party, as each child went through the cinema door, we were given a bag of sweets to eat during the films. At the end of the films, on going out of the door, each child was given a wrapped present and an orange and apple to take home.

On one occasion, as a child, I went to a Pantomime at the Empire Theatre on Newgate Street in Newcastle. Mr and Mrs Stephenson, the greengrocers, took me and Joan, another child from our street to see 'Humpty Dumpty'. We all went in a taxi. As Joan and I got into the taxi we were given a box of chocolates … a Dairy Box.

'We are going to sit in a box, said Mrs Stephenson.

This was a whole new world and we were treated like royalty. It was a special place and almost on the stage. I stared in wonder at the chorus girls lined up dancing in their red short costumes and their black patent leather shoes. We got to go back stage after the show and meet the cast.

Christmas Eve was full of excitement. I and my sisters hung our stocking up on the mantelpiece in the kitchen. A carrot was left for the reindeer then we went to bed. Christmas morning came and we looked first in the now full stockings. Inside was also an orange and an apple – a whole piece of fruit for each of us that we did not have to share. There were some nuts still in their shells that were great fun to break open later. And we received some money … real money … pennies usually. There might also be a new handkerchief or a box of three. The filled stocking was a constant. The one present over the years

A Newcastle Empire Programme.

was different. I was given a doll, a cradle, a pair of skates, Bunty Annuals, a Black Beauty book, a book which showed me how to draw horses. Everything was appreciated by my brothers and sisters.

The Christmas food and treats that were on sale at Laws Stores in the 1950s.

One Christmas I joined the Christmas club. It might have been with my other sisters at the paper shop on Brighton Road. Each week I would take my little card along to the shop and hand over a penny or maybe two and the man would write the amount on the card. By Christmas I had saved enough to buy a present of sweets for each member of my family. There was Bassett Liquorice Allsorts, for Dad and a Dairy Box of chocolates for Mam. To the rest of the family we gave a little chocolate Santa Claus.

On Christmas Eve Mam went to St Chad's Church to the service at midnight. I thought this would be so exciting to go to when I grew up. We all went to the Christmas service in the morning and Rawling Road Methodist Sunday School in the afternoon of Christmas Day. I loved to look at the little Nativity display in church at this time of year.

We would visit Gran and Grandad and some of our aunts on Christmas morning. There were presents of a new handkerchiefs and money. A child could never have too many hankies. This family visiting was always in our Sunday best as it was called – our new best Christmas clothes. Nearly always these clothes for Christmas and the winter months were, for me, a red tartan pleated skirt and a jumper. If needed, I would get a new winter coat. The clothes were always bigger than needed to give room for me to grow into.

Above: An advert for Pepsi from Christmas in the 1950s.

Right: Christmas gifts at bargain prices from R. Pedley, 269 High Street. 'Hopalong and Cinderella Watches' were very popular.

Christmas Day was broken up with dinner. I remember one year before Christmas, I was asleep in bed and Mam burst into the bedroom. 'Look,' she said holding up a huge fresh turkey. 'I won it at the Whist drive, it's for Christmas dinner.'

That turkey lasted forever with turkey dinner, turkey sandwiches, turkey and chips and turkey soup. Mam could make anything go a long way. The following Christmases there was always a fresh turkey. Homemade Christmas pudding followed with Rum sauce. If one of us was lucky we might find a sixpence wrapped in greaseproof paper in the pudding.

Christmas tea was always sandwiches, little cakes, scones and a lovely white decorated Christmas cake. It was always square with a Santa Claus on a sleigh in one corner and a little Christmas tree in another corner. All foods were homemade, well before Christmas. The cake and pudding had to mature so were made well in advance.

The Queen when she visited Gateshead in 1954.

The day these Christmas foods were made was special. I and others would sit at the table watching Mam stirring together the butter and sugar and putting in the dried fruits, spices and adding the eggs. The smell was wonderful and when Mam had finished making the cake or pudding she would let us run our fingers around the bowl and lick the mixture from our fingers. It was delicious and spicy.

There was always a bottle of homemade non-alcoholic Ginger wine. It burnt my mouth but I loved it.

The radio would be on all Christmas day. At 12 noon there were Christmas Family Favourites. Then there was the Queen's speech to listen to on the radio at 3 o'clock. We sat huddled around the roaring red winter fire listening to it all.

There was no playing on Christmas Day as this was a special day. It was a day of rest, a day for going to church and a family day. It was Boxing Day when we could play again with the new toys and things we got for Christmas.

More Memories of Gateshead

The Library

During junior school I joined the local library. This was a small library on the corner of Whitehall Road and Rawling Road. I was thrilled because it cost a penny to join, which was a lot of pocket money for a youngster. Mary, my friend, had joined and she only lived a few doors away so she took me with her.

Every week I would go and borrow a book. Each book had a little pouch stuck into the opening cover and inside this pouch there was a little ticket. The librarian took the ticket out of the book, stamped the return date on it and placed it in a box on her desk. The librarian handed the book to me and reminded me of the date it had to be returned. I could only get one book and I had to take it back to the library after two weeks. If I didn't … then I would have to pay a fine. I always got the book back on time, as it seemed important to me and I would be proud to do so.

I remember as a child taking the book into the big front bedroom to read. I would sit on the bed, sometimes in the cold if the fire wasn't on (meaning there were no babies due to be born).

Mam would come into the room and say, 'Come on our Kathleen, get your nose out of that book and come and set the table.'

We, my sisters and I played libraries. It's what we did – integrate new experiences into play. We would line up some books, create little tickets and stick little pouches inside the front cover of each book. Then we used our little date stamp that came out of a post office set. And hey ho … we had our fun.

Plenty of books inside the Central Library in Gateshead.

Gateshead's Central Library on Prince Consort Road.

Post Office

I think the local post office was at the top of Westminster Street on Rectory Road. So, just like playing at libraries, we then copied playing post offices. I can remember getting a post office set for either Christmas or my birthday. It was a little box that contained envelopes, little stamps, postal orders, a little ink stamp tin and a stamper. They were very popular presents for girls like me.

Swimming

These were the swimming years when all junior children learnt to swim. Each week, with our 'cossies' wrapped in our towels, our class of children walked from school to Shipcote swimming baths. We walked everywhere in those days.

I loved the baths. There were changing rooms with showers which we had to use after the swim to get the chlorine off us. I had never seen showers before in my young life so it was a whole new experience for me.

All children went into the pool at the shallow end. The swimming teacher stood at the front of the pool and called out instructions on what to do. We learnt how to use our arms for the breast stroke by walking along the floor of the pool. To do the leg action we had to hold on to the sides to practice the movement. After a couple of weeks we put the two actions together and, with a lot of practise and courage, I began to swim. Then we practised swimming up and down the pool, from the shallow end to the deep end. Once this was mastered it was how to dive in from a sitting position at the side of the deep end. Eventually I could swim confidently up and down the pool to gain myself the 'quarter of a mile' certificate.

Swimming broadened my horizons. On Saturday mornings during the summer I would walk to the baths at Shipcote with a friend and eventually a sister. After the swim we went to the very small café across the road. There were no tables, maybe a couple of chairs and we never sat down. I would buy myself, if I had any money, a hot drink. This drink was a cup of delicious Oxo … something new to me.

Shipley Art Gallery

We would go along to the Shipley Art Gallery after swimming. Sometimes our class would be taken there to see exhibitions. Just inside the doorway, through a set of glass doors, was a statue of a very large white lion with a naked man sitting on top of it. As we were little, we would giggle at the statue and try to see what we could of the man's nakedness. We would wander around the gallery looking at the pictures, until eventually we would go home.

Near to the Shipley Art Gallery was the main Gateshead Central Library where we would also go, just for a look around, on our swimming trips out. To finish our adventure we would walk back down through the Avenues home. Using our imagination in play, we were home before we realised it.

Right: The statue in the Shipley Art Gallery that fascinated us when we were kids.

Women's work exhibition at Shipley

An exhibition of work done in women's classes in Gateshead, will be held in the Shipley Art Gallery, Prince Consort Road, Gateshead, next Thursday from 2.15 to 8 p.m.; Friday from 10.30 a.m. to 8 p.m. and Saturday also from 10.30 a.m. to 8 p.m.

The exhibition is to be opened by the Mayoress of Gateshead, Mrs. A. Crossley, on Thursday afternoon at 2.15.

A newspaper cutting from the Gateshead Post for a 'Women's work exhibition at Shipley'.

Shipley Art Gallery, Gateshead.

A postcard view of the Shipley Art Gallery.

Town Hall – Plays and Sketches

Another place we visited during these years was the Town Hall. This was a very imposing building to a child and I instinctively knew to behave myself when I went there. Sometimes our class was taken there, maybe on the bus. I remember when we went to see a set of small plays performed by players with Mrs Hetherington, one of the teachers. All the children sat on proper seats set out in rows and in front of us was the stage with closed red curtains. As each play or sketch was to be performed a lady would pop her head out of the closed curtains and announce each sketch with a number for it: 'Item number One ...' then two etc. It was a whole afternoon out of school so great fun.

It was a distance from the Town Hall at the bottom of Gateshead back to school on Brighton Road. I'm not sure if we all walked back to school – all of us in a long caterpillar line holding our partner's hand – or maybe we went back to school on a bus hired for the day. These times gave me a sense of direction and a greater understanding of the area of Gateshead that I lived in.

Gateshead Town Hall – a very impressive building for a child.

Royal Visit

In 1953 Princess Elizabeth was crowned Queen following the death of her father, George VI. The following year, when I was in the junior school about seven years old, the Queen visited Gateshead. A lot of children from the schools in Gateshead were taken to Prince Consort Road and we stood lining the street at the edge of the road. We waved our little Union Jack, red, white and blue flags, as the new Queen and Prince Philip went past in a black car which was part of a longer procession.

Left: Crowds flocked to the Tyne Bridge for the Queen's visit to Tyneside in 1954. Prince Philip is by her side. This was Her Majesty's first visit to the North East after her Coronation the year before. As well as Gateshead, the Queen enjoyed a warm welcome in Newcastle, Sunderland, Wallsend and Tynemouth.

I remember around this time there were National Savings stamps which had the face of Princess Anne or Prince Charles on them. Each Monday morning, children could take sixpence or 2/6 into school and buy a savings stamp. It was sixpence for a Princess Anne stamp and 2/6 for a Prince Charles stamp. We saved them up and to cash them in I went to the Post Office.

Shephard's of Gateshead

We always shopped at Shephard's of Gateshead on West Street – they were a department hent store in a very impressive building. Clothes were bought at Shephard's and I loved it when Mam took me there for new clothes whether summer or winter. Mam would have what was called 'a provi' or 'ticket' and this little chit of paper was from the Provident Insurance Company. The tickets could be purchased from the insurance man who came to our house every Friday to collect the money to be paid back each week. It was credit of the day.

At Shephard's Mam would go to the cash window just inside the store. She handed over the ticket and in exchange she was given different coloured tokens, representing money. The tokens could only be used for buying items in the store.

It was such a big building for a child. I can't remember how many floors there were but I liked to ride in the lift which was like a cage. The lift was a huge thing with railing type doors that had to be pulled across the entrance to close them with a clank. Scary really, but exciting as well!

Right: An advert from Shephard's welcomes the Queen to Gateshead in 1954.

Woolworths

Towards the end of the 1950s, Woolworths on the High Street became another store to visit. My only memory of Woolworths as a child was when I was about 11. The store must have just opened and everything was on display for people to pick up and look at. These items could be taken to be paid for somewhere else in the store. This was a lot different from items being behind a counter that had to be asked for. My friend at that time and I went shopping there. We had more pocket money by this age and should have had more sense. I took a key ring and never paid for it. I later threw it away … and I never went back to Woolworths.

Woolworths on the High Street around 1960. Knotts, another shop I remember, is on the right.

Robson's

I left school at 15 years of age and my very first job was as an office junior at Robson's on the High Street. I enjoyed my time there doing all the cash type jobs. One of my jobs was receiving the money into the office upstairs and this was through the Lamson tube system, which was used in shops and offices to transport small, urgent packages such as mail, paperwork or money over short distances in the building. The cash would be placed in a pod by the shop assistants downstairs then sent along the tubes up to my office. I would take the money out of the pods, count it and enter the amounts in the books. The cash was then put away in the safe.

After the job at Robson's I worked at Hunters the Bakers on the Team Valley Trading Estate. I remember on a Wednesday afternoon, which was my half day off at Robson's, Mam walked me along the Team Valley going into each factory along Kingsway asking if there was a job for an office junior. Eventually at Hunters I got an interview to work in the accounts department. I started work there the following week – I only had to give a week's notice. I worked at Hunter's for two and a half years before going to work at the 'Ministry' at Longbenton.

Right: An advert for M. Robson & Co (Drapers), High Street, Gateshead.

The Team Valley Trading Estate where there was always plenty of work for people in the 1950s. You just had to knock on the doors of each factory until one would give you a job!

End of An Era

During October 1958 a disaster occurred in our street. One evening the row of flats on our side of Westminster Street subsided. The ground seemed to open and swallow the middle group of houses. All the families were evacuated into St Chad's Church Hall and we spent the night there on the floor. The families were looked after by the Women's Royal Voluntary Service (WRVS) with bedding etc provided, as well as food.

The following days were difficult. My two sisters and I spent a few nights sleeping at the house of a neighbour on the other side of Westminster Street. We still all went to school and life went on as normal as possible. Each evening, after school, I would go to my Aunty Doreen's house for tea. This was where Mam stayed with the younger children. Allan, 14 years old by now, was looked after by Aunty Lily and family in Langdon Street. Eventually I went to stay at my friend's house on Whitehall Road for a while. Our Elizabeth stayed with one of her friends also on Whitehall Road. Both of these friends lived opposite to Brighton Avenue School, so easy to go each day.

The story of the street collapse was featured in the Gateshead Post on the 24th October 1958:

GATESHEAD POST
OCTOBER 24, 1958

WESTMINSTER STREET'S
10 p.m. ALARM
12 families had to clear out in a hurry

Right: The newspaper headline from the Gateshead Post.

Below: The article from the Gateshead Post with our family mentioned in the last line.

ON Wednesday night, last week, Westminster Street, Gateshead presented a scene of chaos, as men, women and children milled into the streets after their homes began caving in around them.

It was just after 10 o'clock at night when cracks

On Wednesday night, last week, Westminster Street, Gateshead presented a scene of chaos, as men, women and children milled into the streets, after their homes began caving in around them. It was just after 10 o'clock at night when cracks, four inches wide, zig-zagged down bedroom and living room walls, simultaneously in all the flats, from number 91 up the street to number 117. Houses from 89 to the bottom of the street were unaffected.

Twelve families were immediately evacuated from their houses which threatened to tumble around them at any moment, and with others, were temporarily housed at nearby St Chad's Church hall. Tea and meals were served them by the WRVS members of the Welfare of the Civil Defence Corps.

Some families went straight to families and friends for the night. Others were cared for in Corporation Hostels. Babies and young children were taken to nearby nurseries. Police and Civil Defence officials were in attendance to the old, sick and nursing mothers all through the night. Gas and electricity supplies were cut off as a precaution.

The Lord Mayor of Gateshead Alderman J.W. Roberts arrived on the scene and called a meeting of the families in the church hall. He asked them to co-operate with welfare officials. Many of the residents had only recently re-furnished and papered rooms of their 24s a week flats and some had decorated them throughout.

Subsidence of old colliery workings was believed to be the cause of collapsing of the houses. Even two houses numbers 100 and 102 Hyde Park Street, which runs adjacent to Westminster Street, have been slightly affected.

Mrs E. Henderson told the Gateshead Post that her brother-in-law, Mr F. Bell at 91 Westminster Street, called her after 10 o'clock on Wednesday night and told her the walls and ceilings were cracking around him and his wife and family of a boy and a month old baby. Plaster was falling in piles around them he said. Ceilings were sagging so much that their weight was bending bolts on the doors. Mr Bell was cleaning his teeth in the scullery when a large piece of plaster fell from the ceiling onto his head. Other residents told similar stories.

Eighteen year old Harry Proudlock of 93, an upstairs flat, said he had just got to bed at about 10.15 when his father, Mr James Proudlock, shouted for him. He saw cracks, two and three inches wide visibly appearing in the walls of the living room which they had only redecorated a week before. Together his father and he dashed into one of the front bedrooms and dragged the five girls of the family who were sleeping together from the bed, seconds before half of the bedroom ceiling caved in on to the bed. Mrs Proudlock and her other four sons including a young baby were quickly hustled out of another front bedroom. The family were scattered all over with friends and neighbours and in nurseries.

Mr J. Bright, at number 99, is rather less lucky than the rest of the residents in the street because he owns the house he lives in and it, like the rest, is almost completely ruined. Mr Bright is another who had completely re-decorated recently only to have his work undone.

Clearing up in Westminster Street after the subsidence.

The house at the top of Westminster Street which is a gable end flat, although evacuated wasn't as extensively damaged as the rest on Wednesday, but on Friday the gable end wall was visibly sagging outwards onto a back lane.

Late on Thursday evening of last week Gateshead Corporation were still working in the dusk removing the last of the furniture from the flats into corporation vans to various storing places in Gateshead, after it had been carefully checked and labelled by welfare workers. And on Friday a meeting was called at the welfare centre, Prince Consort Road, Gateshead, which was attended by representatives of the Town Clerk's Borough Surveyor's, Welfare Services, Children's and Housing Departments and a member of each of the evacuated houses, to discuss more permanent housing matters.

The 12 evacuated families involving 59 people are: number 91 Westminster Street, Mr & Mrs F. Bell; 93, Mr & Mrs J. Proudlock, and 10 children; 95, Mrs Ayres and child; 97, Mr & Mrs A. Coulthard and two children; 99, Mr & Mrs J. Bright and two children; 101, Mr & Mrs Burns; 103, Mr & Mrs McKay; 105, Mr & Mrs Trotter and three children; 107, a women and her niece; Mrs Forster & Miss Hedley; 109, Mr & Mrs J. Robson and eight children; 115, Mr & Mrs Jones and seven children; 117, Mr & Mrs W. Reilly and child.

A group of children watch the scene in Westminster Street in 1958. A number of families in the street had to be re-housed and they went to live at Leam Lane or Carr Hill Estates – the new council housing estates in Gateshead. We returned to our flat for a few months. It wasn't as damaged as others because we were on the end, near the back lane. Eventually in 1959 we were re-housed on the Lyndhurst Estate at Low Fell. Thus, the end of my childhood memories of Gateshead in the 1950s.

Acknowledgements

The author would like to thank the following who have kindly helped with this book:

John Harrison, Allan Jones, Elizabeth Stevens, Peter Annable, George Nairn

The Chronicle, Gateshead Libraries, Newcastle Libraries, Tyne & Wear Archives

A wonderful photograph of a tram on its way to Bensham and a nice image to end this journey through my childhood.

Also available from Summerhill Books

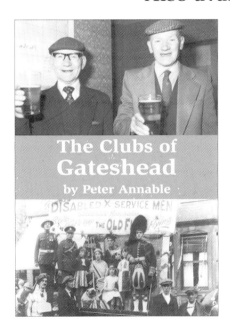

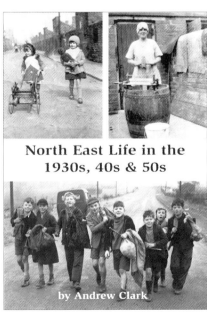

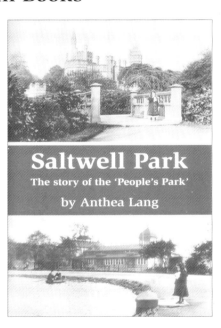

visit our website to view our full range of books
www.summerhillbooks.co.uk